Let'n Went!

For my brothers B & M
who participated in many of the
incidents narrated, but who prefer
to remain anonymous

Crumps Barn Studio
Crumps Barn, Syde, Cheltenham GL53 9PN
www.crumpsbarnstudio.co.uk

Cover design by Lorna Gray
Plan of Fern Cottage by Lorna Gray
All photographs © Ceri Vyner 2022

Printed in Gloucestershire on FSC certified paper by SevernPrint, a carbon neutral company

ISBN 978-1-915067-14-2

Let'n Went!

CERI VYNER

A Memoir

Crumps Barn Studio

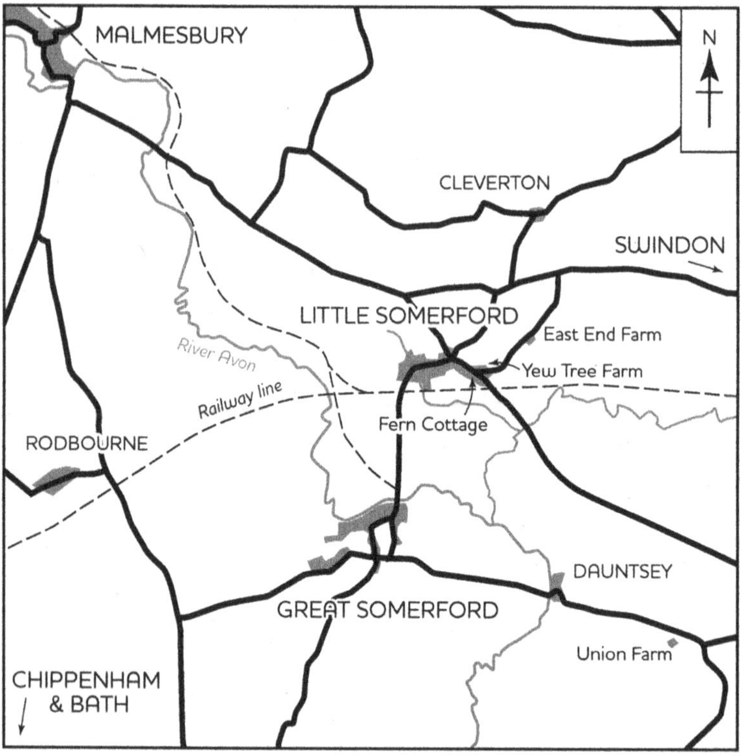

Map of Little Somerford and nearby towns c.1950 (not to scale)

INTRODUCTION

THE VILLAGE

Wiltshire is an inland county in South West England, bordered on all sides by the counties of Gloucestershire, Oxfordshire, Berkshire, Hampshire, Dorset and Somerset. Its countryside includes rolling chalk downlands, and Salisbury Plain in the south of the county. The northern part is characterised by attractive villages built of the local creamy-gold limestone. The houses blend beautifully into the surrounding countryside and over many years develop a soft, luminous colour as if the sunlight has soaked into the stones.

Little Somerford was, before modern development, an exceptionally pretty village in North Wiltshire. Situated on the southern edge of the Cotswolds, it lies in a fertile valley between the River Avon on one side and Brinkworth Brook, a tributary of the Avon, on the other. It is a nucleated village set in undulating countryside and green meadows. Small mixed farms with cattle, a few pigs or sheep, and poultry meant that the old meadows were seldom ploughed then and contained many varieties of wild flowers. The smell of sweet meadow hay scented the whole village at harvest time. In some fields the old ridge and furrow could clearly be seen.

The main road from Malmesbury to Swindon runs along the ridge of the escarpment and was built on chalk, but down in the valley, the geology is fertile soil on clay. One steep road running from Somerford Corner up to the main road at the top of the escarpment is called Clay Street.

The most important houses and the Church of St John the Baptist are in The Street (recently re-named Park Lane). These include Somerford House and Manor Farm, both built of Cotswold Stone with stone tiled roofs. There is also a lovely Queen Anne style former rectory built of red brick with a stone pillared porch, next to the church. Within a short distance of these were a school, shop, public house and garage (formerly the forge). They were all at the heart of village life.

There were eight small, mixed farms in the village in the 1950s. Council houses were built on the Great Somerford end of the village in the 1930s. In 1961 the Census revealed that there were 232 people in the village, but this increased with the building of the Vale Leaze housing estate in the 1960s and by 1971 the population was 351. The village was a real community, and everybody knew everybody very well.

The new South Wales railway line was opened in 1903 and the new section was known as *The New Direct*. When it was built, a station was created at Little Somerford. A viaduct carried the line over the River Avon and small tunnels were built under the track so that cattle could access the further fields on their farms. The line was built by navvies for whom several railway cottages were built at each end of the village. Some navvies stayed on after the railway was completed, doing odd jobs and helping with the harvest on village farms. Others worked on the railway as linesmen or platelayers. The branch line which ran between Dauntsey, Great Somerford and Malmesbury divided as it passed Little Somerford in Mill Lane, where there was a level crossing and gatekeeper's cottage. This line was altered in 1933 so that the branch line began at Little Somerford. A favourite outing when we were very small children was to walk down through the village and along Mill Lane to watch Bill Archard the gate keeper as he closed the level crossing gates. We would wave to the train as it went through the level crossing and chat to Bill as he opened the gates again.

The market town of Malmesbury is three miles away and most shopping was done there. During the 1950s and 1960s buses provided an hourly service to Malmesbury. One bus came from Chippenham every two hours, stopping to pick up passengers just past Somerford Corner outside the old Kings Head public house. For many years this was driven by a very kind driver called Bob. The other bus travelled from Swindon to Malmesbury and back, picking up or dropping off passengers on the main road near the top of Little Somerford Hill. People would have to walk down The Hill into the village. On one occasion I was on the bus when a lady with four heavy bags of groceries wanted to get off at Lea, a village halfway between Malmesbury and Little Somerford. The bus stop was only on the edge of the village. 'Hang on a minute, dear,' said the driver, kindly, eyeing her bags of shopping. 'Anybody mind if we go down 'ere?' he called out. Since nobody objected, he turned the bus off its route and drove a good half mile down the lane into Lea where he dropped the lady off outside her house before turning round and resuming his usual route. He would not be allowed to do that these days, but we were a community then.

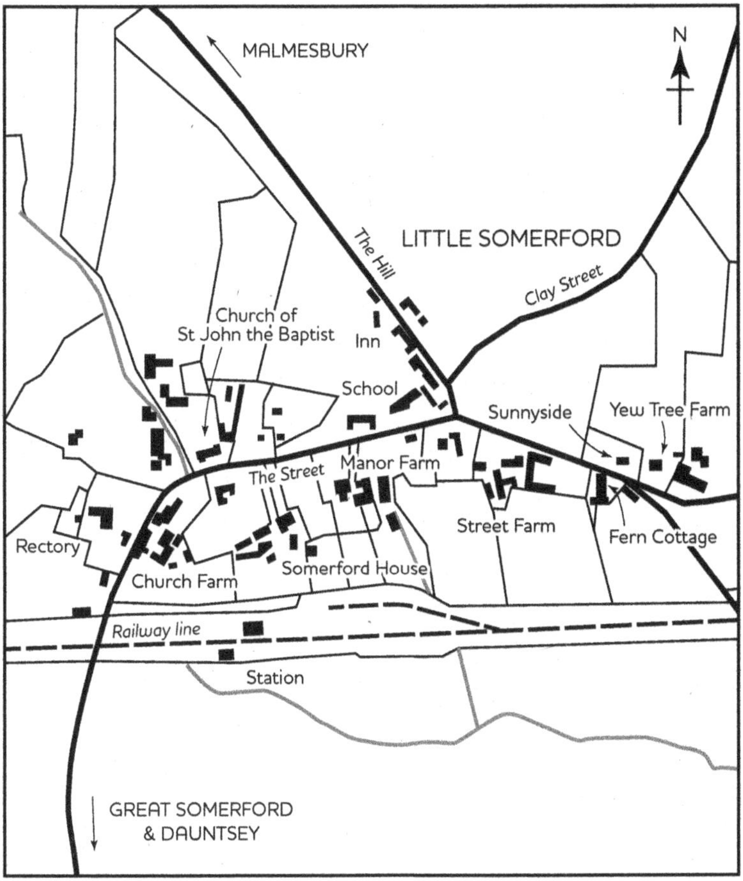

Map of Little Somerford c.1950 (not to scale)

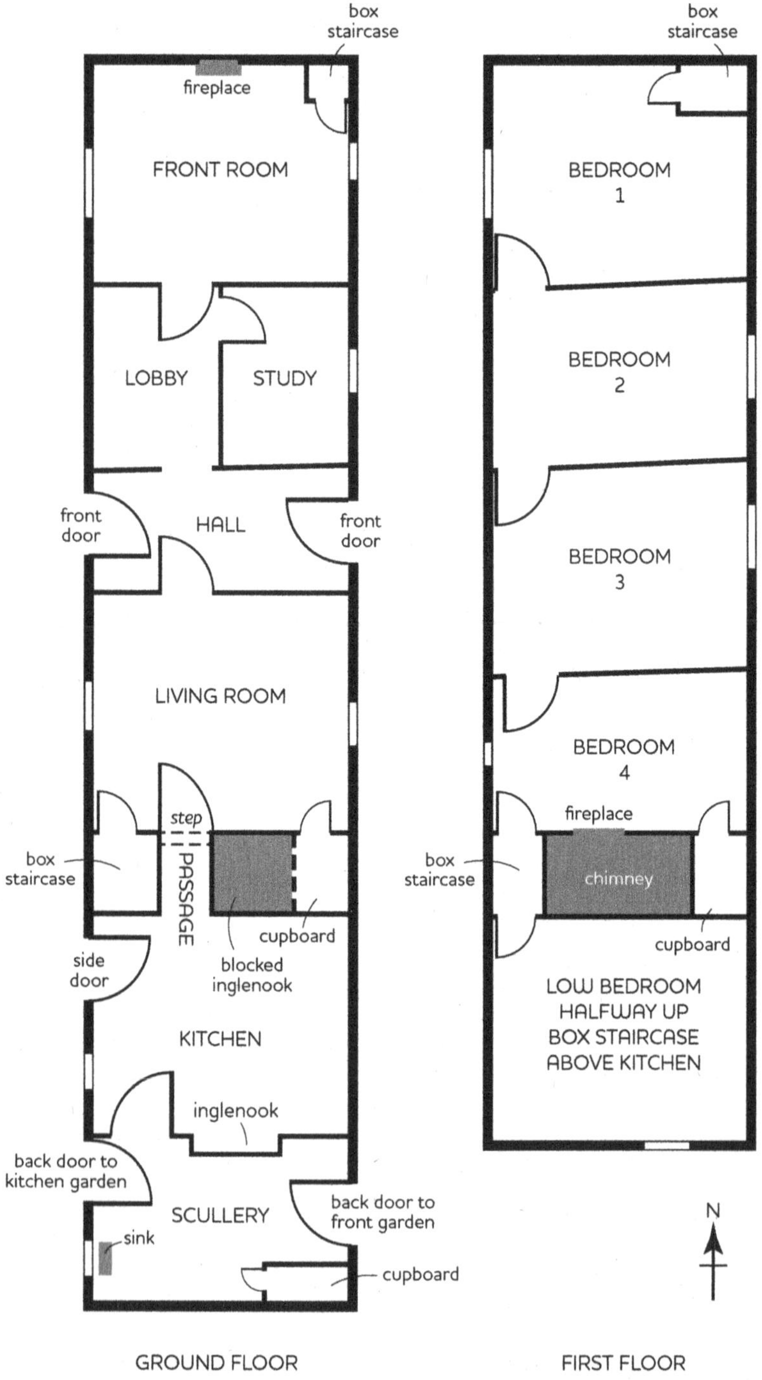
box staircase
fireplace
FRONT ROOM
LOBBY
STUDY
front door
HALL
front door
LIVING ROOM
step
box staircase
PASSAGE
cupboard
side door
blocked inglenook
KITCHEN
inglenook
back door to kitchen garden
SCULLERY
back door to front garden
sink
cupboard
box staircase
BEDROOM 1
BEDROOM 2
BEDROOM 3
BEDROOM 4
fireplace
box staircase
chimney
cupboard
LOW BEDROOM HALFWAY UP BOX STAIRCASE ABOVE KITCHEN
N
GROUND FLOOR
FIRST FLOOR

CHAPTER 1

THE COTTAGE

It is more than forty years since I left my old home at Little Somerford, but my memories of it and the beautiful village in which it stood are vivid in my mind.

Our family – Father, Mother, my two older brothers and myself – arrived in Little Somerford in February 1954 when I was fourteen months old. We had lived in a little village near Bath, but the house was too small for a growing family. My mother had instigated the move to Little Somerford by answering an advertisement in a local newspaper, offering a cottage for rent. Several other local people also wanted The Cottage, but the owners, the Reeves, who farmed at Yew Tree Farm just up the road, wanted a family with young children to live there and bring more life into the village and we were the chosen ones. Our house was known for many years as The Cottage, but our landlords, the Reeves, found that name unacceptable on official forms, so it was later renamed Fern Cottage after the ferns which grew by the front door.

My two brothers, B aged nearly five, and M aged

three, had arrived earlier in the removal van with my father. They were welcomed by two of the Reeve brothers who greeted them, handed over the large key and informed them that two cats, Susan, a tortoiseshell, and Pickle, a black cat, were in residence and went with the cottage. My mother, grandmother and I arrived by bus a little later. My first memory of the house is of flickering firelight reflecting off the cottage walls as I was carried round in my grandmother's arms as she and my mother inspected our new home.

The cottage was long and almost divided the garden into two. It was built largely of mellow red brick, apart from the kitchen end which was stone and slightly lower than the rest of the house. The roof was of charcoal grey Bridgewater tiles and the old walls had two tie bars with S shaped ends. It had once been two cottages so it had two front doors and two back doors. There was also a side door leading directly into the kitchen, but we rarely used it.

At one end of the house there was a room with a door beside the fireplace opening onto the box staircase. On the opposite side of this room another door opened onto a dark lobby, the window of which had been filled in. A small partitioned room was at one side of the lobby and an open doorway led from the lobby into a flagstoned hallway with a front door at each side. The yellow flagstones here were of a better quality than those in the rest of the house.

A side door opened from the hall into the living room. At one time this living room would have had a large inglenook, but this had been blocked off in Victorian times and a small fireplace created. On one side of the fireplace were two deep cupboards, one above the other, and on the opposite side were two latched doors. One door revealed two steps and a narrow flagged passage along the side of the inglenook. The other door opened onto box staircase.

The short passage leading from the living room into the kitchen was so low that anyone over four feet high had to bend almost double in order to go through it and my father, who was over six feet four inches tall, only managed it by a sideways crab-like scuttle.

Through the passage was a kitchen with a beamed ceiling and a flagged floor of grey and red coarse sandstone flagstones. This housed a large black range from beneath which fearsome Devil's coach horse beetles emerged in search of crumbs or other food. A small blocked up window space with three shelves served as a display area for china, and a large wooden cupboard was used as a larder and store.

Tacked on to the kitchen was a lean-to scullery with an asbestos roof. At one end was a butler's sink with one cold water tap and a wooden draining board beneath the small window. Two high wooden shelves ran along the end wall above the side of the sink. This was where my mother kept a bar of household soap and a packet of Daz washing powder. Part of the scullery had been converted into a lavatory with a portable Elsan bucket with a seat on top. For some reason we never used this – I expect it leaked. Instead, since the house was not on mains drainage, we used the two privies near the back doors.

Each room led into the next and if you opened the inside scullery door, the two living room doors and the door to the end room, you could see right through the house.

Upstairs there was a large low room over the kitchen which had once been a servant's room. Then there were four other rooms all leading into one another with the furthest one having a door to the box staircase at the other end of the house. These were our bedrooms.

Outside, on one side of the house was a very attractive front garden and on the other a large, well-stocked kitchen garden.

There was a door at each end of the scullery leading to the front and back (kitchen) gardens. The door to the kitchen garden opened onto a covered area between the house and an old washhouse. The washhouse had an old-fashioned copper in one corner. This had a grate underneath so that the copper could be filled with water and a fire lit underneath it. This would provide hot water for baths or washing clothes. Also in the washhouse was a large tin bath which was brought into the kitchen once a week and partially filled with water for our baths. The old pump was sited outside the washhouse, but we were warned not to drink the water as it was unhealthy. The Reeves told us that before the mains water was connected, the Slopers, who lived in The Cottage then, had to collect drinking water from Street Farm every day.

There was also an old stable which was used as a coal shed and store, and in a small building just beyond the house were the privies. These earth closets were housed in a double shed, back-to-back, and each privy had two holes cut in the seat! Every six months or so they had to be dug out and their contents buried in a deep hole in some part of the garden. This probably accounted for the black, fertile soil and the flourishing kitchen garden. The village was not on mains drainage until the 1960s and our house for some reason was never connected, so my father refused to pay the sewerage part of his water bill. The water company took him to court, but their case was dismissed and we never did pay the sewerage rate.

CHAPTER 2

HOME

Our parents were cultured, but not at all well off and the house was sparsely furnished. They appreciated art, literature, antiques, ballet, music and history and encouraged us to take an interest in these. Our father was passionate about books, and the lobby and end room were lined with books in rickety bookcases, so much so that a friend of M's visiting in the 1960s remarked: 'Well, M, if I hadn't known this was your house, I'd have thought it was the public library!'

At home we were expected to speak standard English with no Wiltshire accent and our parents were well spoken. At the village school we were teased because our mother 'talked posh.'

'Your mum dun't talk like our mums, do she?'

'Yes, she does.'

'No she dun't, she dun't talk ordinary, she talk posh!'

We had a small number of pictures which came from our paternal grandmother's family: a small Mersey river scene, a view of Bath and a pair of Scottish landscapes, one of which became the accidental target of an arrow fired from a homemade bow, and for many years had a hole in the canvas.

The living room walls were painted in a soft, straw-coloured distemper which rubbed off on our clothes when we brushed against it. The woodwork was initially white, but turned a dirty yellow after years of absorbing the smoke from my father's Players cigarettes. The room was dominated by a large mahogany sideboard on legs, a relic of our grandmother's house. As a small child I often crouched underneath it, peering out at my family enjoying their third pot of tea at Saturday breakfast. I shared the space with the family mongrel, a hound-cross female dog called Timmy, who used the front edge of the sideboard as a convenient scratching post to ease the irritation of fleas on her back. From here Timmy was ready to dart out to receive the occasional scrap of food passed down to her. On one memorable occasion my father was shaking the brown sauce bottle to move the contents to the top of it. As he jerked it down sharply poor Timmy darted out from under the sideboard and instead of receiving the expected titbit, was whacked on the head and cried piteously, and had to be comforted and consoled with half a rasher of bacon.

A table and chairs, one easy chair in the corner by the fire, and a Tricity Viscount paraffin stove furnished the living room. The floor was of worn bare oak boards with just a small hearth rug in front of the fire. A radio, a Carnival ware bowl with iridescent green glass, and a vase of garden flowers stood on the sideboard. A Derby jug and an alarm clock were set on the mantelpiece.

These were used as weights to hold down damp garments drying over the fire.

During our first few years at The Cottage we used the old Victorian range for cooking, but eventually it needed a spare part which we were unable to obtain and it fell into disuse. Thereafter the paraffin stove in the living room was the only form of heating in the house as although there was a grate in the front room at the far end of the house, it was only lit at Christmas for a few days.

We did not have many toys. There were a few toy bricks and some Britains farm animals which I played with when I was small. My brothers had a few Dinky toy cars which they would not let me play with. We each had a teddy: mine was a panda which was never the same after I played 'doctors' with him and cut him open to remove his squeak! B later had a small Meccano set and made cranes and various vehicles. M was keen on cowboys and had toy cap guns and a belt with a holster. Both of my brothers had spud guns which fired pieces of potato which stung my face and arms. I could only retaliate with a water pistol. B was keen on Airfix models of aeroplanes which had to be glued together. In summer we preferred more active games such as cricket which was played with a tennis ball and a homemade bat. We all collected cigarette cards and the sets of cards which came in Brook Bond tea.

When we were of primary school age, we all loved Transfers. These were issued in perforated sheets, rather like large rectangular postage stamps. The images included birds, flowers, butterflies, cars, lorries, aeroplanes and dinosaurs.

They cost two pennies per half sheet or four pennies for a whole one. When I was about nine the prices increased to three pence and six pence respectively.

The Transfers were carefully separated and given out one or two at a time by our mother. Each Transfer had to be dipped into cold water until thoroughly soaked and then applied face downwards onto the backs of our hands or lower arms and pressed down firmly. After an impatient wait of about two or three minutes, the backing paper could be peeled back and the image proudly displayed.

I loved the pretty butterflies best, but my brothers always clamoured for cars or dinosaurs, so I often had to make do with these. Transfers were only allowed on Saturday mornings or school holidays as our mother insisted on all Transfers being scrubbed off before school.

These days children have stickers instead, but I still think the Transfers were more fun, as well as teaching children patience, because if the backing was peeled off too soon the Transfer was spoilt or smudged.

We had no television, but the radio was a constant companion in the evenings and for part of the weekend. After primary school we would rush home to listen to Children's Hour. *Carbonel,* the adventures of *Norman and Henry Bones, Polly and Oliver*, and *The Hobbit* were all favourites. We all loved listening *to The Clitheroe Kid, The Navy Lark* and *Top of the Form*. As we grew older, *Saturday Night Theatre and The Paul Temple Mysteries* were a feature of our Saturday evenings. At Sunday lunches, we had to consume our puddings in silence as our mother listened to *Gardeners' Question Time.* On Sunday evenings after I had gone to bed, the sounds of *Sing Something Simple* or *Your Hundred Best Tunes* drifted up through the floorboards.

From the age of six we spent much of our time outside for most of the year, retreating into the house from November to March, and playing endless games of rummy and Monopoly and reading everything which came our way.

We were all omnivorous readers. *Winnie the Pooh, Milly Molly Mandy, Thomas the Tank Engine* and the Little Grey Rabbit books had been read to us in our infancy. As we grew older we loved the Jennings books, Billy Bunter, Malcolm Saville's *Lone Pine* series and especially the *Romney Marsh* and *Punchbowl Farm* adventures by Monica Edwards, which were read repeatedly throughout our schooldays.

We were encouraged to read the legends of King Arthur and tales of Robin Hood, Rosemary Sutcliffe's wonderful historical adventures, and fantasy stories such as *The Hobbit*, and *The Weirdstone of Brisingamen. The Wind in the Willows* and *Tom's Midnight Garden* were read repeatedly when we were confined to bed with mumps or flu.

We were allowed to read anything which our parents considered 'good' literature. They did not approve of the Enid Blyton stories or The Beano and Dandy comics, but we read them anyway, borrowing them from friends and reading them under the bedclothes by torchlight.

We all read The Eagle, and when I was nine a new comic called Princess was issued which I was allowed to have. We all enjoyed this and even our parents read some of it. Our reading was extremely varied; by the age of eleven I might often read *Jane Eyre* or *The Mill on the Floss*, Georgette Heyer's historical romances, Monica Edwards's children's adventure stories and part of *The Lord of the Rings* in the same fortnight as these were all favourite books.

CHAPTER 3

THE GARDEN

I was not the only one to think the garden beautiful, for strangers sometimes stopped their cars and wandered around it, peering through the cottage windows and startling my mother. It was surrounded by tall hedges of privet and hawthorn and almost divided in two by the rambling house which had once been two cottages.

The front garden was formally laid out, with flower beds set in the lawn which had two rose arches up the centre, leading the eye to the clumps of lilac beyond.

An ancient apple tree leaned over the hedge with an air of an anxious mother looking for a sight of her children. The tree cropped profusely, as did everything in that garden, the apples being fragrant, strongly flavoured and excellent keepers. Beside the apple tree grew an enormous box bush. Clipped into a round ball it made a good hiding place for children if one did not mind the earwigs and woodlice which lived beneath it. During snowy weather it resembled a large Christmas pudding with sauce on top.

In winter, half the village changed their walks just

to see our snowdrops, and neighbours admitted that they had never seen so many in one cottage garden. They flowed from the hedge bank like a tide, an army of green spears surrounding the garden, and gathering in a snowy mass under the lilacs until winter's surrender. Even earlier than the snowdrops, the sinister yellow aconites appeared under the apple tree, their jesters' collars belying the poison within.

Forsythia, apple, hawthorn, lilac and laburnum followed one after another, each one coming into its own as the previous one declined. Great clumps of white bells, which the locals called 'white bluebells' grew in the flower beds, and lupins, purple vetch and sweet rocket, growing in profusion amongst the weeds, were later followed by Michaelmas daisies, Japanese anemones and golden rod.

The vine, which clothed the side of the house, sent green tendrils in at the windows above the delicately scented sweet peas which grew in the shelter of the sunny wall. Lavender bushes leaned drunkenly over the edge of the border onto the crazy paving of the path where white arabis, aubretia and old fashioned columbines, which country children call 'granny bonnets', disputed with the weeds for the sunniest spots between the stones. Even the stones themselves were interesting, being irregular in shape and surface and each one, if it were turned over, showing itself to be the shelter of hundreds of scurrying brown ants.

An old Williams pear tree stood against the end wall of the house facing the gate. Early primroses flowered here amongst the uneven paving where the house provided protection from the wind. Nearby, an old stone sink, later planted with pansies and trailing lobelia, gave shelter for the toad which lived under its dank shade. The hedge was thicker here and entangled with rambling Albertine roses. The snowberries from this part of the hedge were carefully collected by us children and thrown into the road where they gave a satisfying pop when squashed by passing cars.

The kitchen garden on the other side of the house was divided into four by grass paths. Enclosed and protected by thick privet and hawthorn hedges, it was a favourite nesting place for thrushes and blackbirds. Exotic peonies with their dark, glossy leaves and brilliant flowers basked in the afternoon sun. Standard roses and phlox flanked the laden Victoria plum tree by the front door, while the honeysuckle and summer jasmine growing up the house walls scented the air. Thick clumps of tall rudbeckia daises almost obscured the light from the living room window and people inside the house seemed to be looking into a green cave.

Gooseberry bushes grew along the edges of the vegetable patches. The small green gooseberries were generally sour and only good when cooked, but the large dessert gooseberries ripened to a dark red colour and burst on the tongue, filling the mouth with sweetness. Thick clumps of rhubarb provided welcome shade for the house cats on hot summer days and from here they were able to guard the strawberries and raspberries from marauding birds.

At right angles to the house stood the old wash house. Virginia creeper had laid claim to it years ago and in autumn its orange bricks and terracotta coloured tiles were transformed to a soft glowing red. Beside the wash house grew a tangle of red, white and black currant bushes. Rarely cut back and never sprayed, they flourished on the black fertile soil and cropped abundantly. Near them, against the wash house wall was the compost heap. This was sometimes home to grass snakes which were attracted by the warmth.

Beyond that was the old stable, sadly now just home to the dustbin and a pile of firewood. Bluetits nested in cracks in its walls and the sun-bleached door still bore the initials WD, neatly carved by a previous owner. Inside in its cobwebby darkness one might fancy that one could hear the echo of hooves and the contented munching of former horses.

We grew nearly all the vegetables we needed in three large plots. The other section was overshadowed by an enormous quince tree. I both loved and feared the quince tree. I loved the beautiful twisted branches, especially when highlighted by winter snow. I admired the delicately scented white blossom in spring. The deep yellow fruits had a pearly white bloom on them which, when touched, became like a handful of thick, grey dust. Their unforgettable scent seemed the essence of autumn to me and no autumn will ever be the same without them, but the moon shining through the twisted branches combined with the light switch on my wall to make a grotesque, grinning face, which terrified me and gave me fearful dreams.

Beside the quince tree grew a tall pear tree. Its fruits ripened early and were particularly sweet and juicy and there was great competition between the children of the house and the wasps as to who could get them first.

In winter when the flowers had died and rows of sprouts stood like sentinels against the bitter wind, the bare earth would yield its own unique crop of old china shards, clay pipe fragments and clay marbles. The garden that once was still haunts my dreams and no season will ever be the same again.

CHAPTER 4

TEA AT UNION FARM

The Reeves had farmed at Little Somerford for many years and after the First World War two of the Reeve brothers rented Union Farm at Dauntsey, the next village, and one of their sisters went with them to keep house.

I first met John, William and Eliza (Lizzie) Reeve in the 1950s when I was three years old and we were invited to tea at Union Farm. This was a very unusual occurrence – the Reeve family were very private.

Our first visit came about because the brothers and sisters at Yew Tree Farm at Little Somerford had quarrelled with their siblings at Union Farm, and they had been hardly on speaking terms for the previous seven or eight years. Then Lizzie, the sister at Union Farm became very ill. Nellie Reeve, from Yew Tree Farm, came to call on my mother.

'I feel I ought to go down. Those two old men won't know what to pack for my poor sister when she goes into hospital. Come down with me and have tea.' Then she added, 'My brothers are rather shy, they won't speak to you, but if you ask a question they will answer.'

My mother only found out later about the rift in the family, and realized that she had been invited to keep the peace as the Reeves would not dream of quarrelling if a stranger was present.

Lizzie Reeve could no longer keep house for her brothers, so Kate and Nellie at Yew Tree Farm had to bake bread, pies, cakes and puddings and take them down to Union Farm each week. My mother insisted that she could only come to tea if she brought us children as well as we were too young to be left alone, so we were included in the invitation.

First we had to have our hands and faces scrubbed at the sink in the scullery, put on clean jumpers and be reminded to be on our best behaviour. It was a two and a half mile trek down the road, over the humpbacked bridge over the brook and down to Idover, a hamlet between Little Somerford and Dauntsey, where we entered the gates of Dauntsey Park. After a walk of about a mile across the park we crossed the river again and turned the corner to Union Farm. We took the old pram with us because, at only three years old, I was rather tired on the journey home and the pram could also be loaded with fallen branches which we used for fuel.

My brothers and I loved going to Union Farm although we had to be very well behaved. First there was tea. We always sat at a low table near the fire while the men sat at the big kitchen table a few feet away. Nellie and Kate Reeve would normally serve the tea. Two wafer thin slices of bread and butter had to be eaten in silence.

This was always a bit of an ordeal, especially for me, as I was apt to get fits of the giggles which would be seriously frowned upon and a punishable offence later at home.

Lizzie Reeve, who was now an invalid, sat in a high-backed armchair. Her hands shook constantly and she drank her tea out of an invalid cup which had a spout, and it seemed to me that she was drinking out of a teapot and this made me giggle even more.

Halfway through our tea the men would come in from milking or haymaking: John Reeve and his elder brother William, and Walter, a local man who helped on the farm – tall lean men with weathered faces from years of outdoor work.

They dressed in striped collarless shirts, waistcoats, trousers and flat caps, the uniform of the Victorian farmer. They would often be in a hurry, so would pour their tea into deep saucers and drink it with loud slurps, followed by gusty sighs of satisfaction which would cause us great amusement and we would shake with laughter. A warning look from our mother would generally calm us down enough to be able to finish our slice of fruit or sponge cake, whereupon we would be sent out into the yard to amuse ourselves while the family talked 'business'. Over the next few days further fun would be had as my brothers would imitate the slurping and breathy sighs of the tea drinkers.

The Reeves all referred to me as *The Little Maid.* At first I was offended.

'They think I'm a servant,' I complained to my mother.

'No they don't,' she replied.

'Yes, they do. They call me The Little Maid.'

'It doesn't mean that, it's just an old-fashioned term for a little girl,' laughed my mother.

'Oh!' After that explanation I didn't mind.

My mother, of course, reported this conversation back to the Reeves who were all highly amused by my mistake.

It was on one of these visits to the Reeves that M shut me in the stable with the big carthorse, Blackbird. B, our elder brother, was not with us on this occasion so M and I were on our own. We had been let out into the yard after our tea and we looked around for something to entertain us.

First, we leaned over the low wall of the pigsty and watched the pigs grunting in satisfaction over the last slops in their trough.

'What's in here?' asked M as he slid open the door of the barn and we peered in. The cows were all out in their field, there was just a lingering milky smell of cows coupled with an odour of cow dung. Shutting the barn door again, M dragged an empty bucket over to the stable. He upended it and climbed onto it, stretching to reach the bolt on the lower half of the stable door. Pulling the bucket back, he opened the door a little way and suddenly shoved me inside and I heard the bolt being drawn shut behind me.

As I stumbled into the stable, propelled by the sharp push from M, I heard a man's voice saying urgently:

'Stop! Stop! Stand still, stand still, he won't hurt you if you stand still.'

I'm sure this voice was my Guardian Angel, as there was no adult in the farmyard at all. I obeyed the voice and stood still, trying to make sense, in the dim light, of the large back legs of the carthorse with their soft hairy feathering just above the hooves. Its hind quarters loomed high above me, a darker shadow in the gloom. A rustling noise made me look up and as my eyes adjusted to the gloom of the stable I gasped in surprise at the enormous animal towering above me.

The carthorse stopped chewing for a moment and turned his head to look me over carefully. As I was standing still, he turned back to his hay net and began eating again. Luckily for me, standing by the enormous hooves, carthorses are gentle beasts and although about eighteen hands high, Blackbird was no exception. I stood quietly watching him pulling mouthfuls of the sweet meadow hay from the net and chomping contentedly.

Soon, I heard John Reeve ask M where I was. I didn't dare call out as I was anxious not to disturb Blackbird. M pretended he didn't know I was in the stable, but after searching the yard John Reeve looked over the high half door and I heard a startled exclamation of surprise and shock. He hastily drew back the bolt and holding himself in line with the wall he reached in, stretching his arm out to me and quietly reminded me to be careful so that I should not touch the huge horse unexpectedly and startle him. He swiftly drew me out to safety before bolting the stable door firmly.

‘Reckon you’ll be safer indoors,’ he said, looking down at me anxiously, and holding my small hand firmly he led me towards the farmhouse.

‘Right under that horse’s belly, she was,’ he exclaimed as we entered the kitchen where everyone was sitting. ‘Dunno ’ow she survived; she was right by his back hooves.’

‘But how could she get in there, she’s much too small to reach the bolt.’ said Kate.

‘M must’ve put ‘er in there! Was it M?’ he asked me.

I nodded, still feeling shocked at my ordeal.

‘Well, what a naughty boy!’ exclaimed Kate. ‘He ought to be punished for that’ she added, glancing at my mother.

‘Oh, she hasn’t come to any harm,’ laughed my mother.

‘Nevertheless, it’s a very dangerous thing to do!’ she replied.

I was praised for being sensible and rewarded with a biscuit, because, they reasoned, it must have been a very frightening experience for such a small child.

Then came the long trek home in the summer dusk, warm and mothy; our legs tired with that healthy tiredness that promised a deep sleep.

CHAPTER 5

ROYAL BRITISH LEGION PARTIES

During the early 1950s there were children's parties held in our area which were run by The Royal British Legion. Little Somerford used to combine with Great Somerford, Brinkworth and Crudwell for these events. The party took place in early January and was held alternately in Little Somerford Village Hall or Crudwell Village Hall. Coaches were laid on to ferry everyone to and fro. A team of ladies prepared the food and the men ran the games.

We would arrive at the village hall in the early afternoon. All the children from each village would be invited and the noise in the hall was deafening to begin with. After hanging up our coats we would sit cross legged on the floor while we were organised into teams for the games.

There was a whole series of party games involving balloons, balls and bean bags, with prizes for the winning teams and a sweet for the losers. The aim was obviously to tire us children out so that we would be calmer for the tea party. There were lots of relay races where we had to race up and down to collect a bean bag from a bucket, run back to our team and sit down before the next team member could start. Another game involved a ball being rolled through the legs of the entire team, with the person at the end catching the ball and running to the front to have their turn. Balloons were passed between the knees or held under our chins and passed to the next team member without touching it with our hands or dropping it. It is surprising how much fun was had from these simple games, and all the time there were the shouts and screams of the participants as they egged on their fellow team members or cheered them to victory.

Then, at last, it was time for tea, and what a tea it was. Trestle tables were laid out with plates of sandwiches, fancy cakes, sausage rolls, cheese straws, jam tarts and coloured jellies in paper cases. I had never seen anything like it.

Crackers were handed out too, and we all wore our coloured paper hats and examined and compared the little cracker toys.

On one occasion when I was five, I found myself sitting opposite a slightly older girl called Georgina, and her younger brother Somerville. I had not met them before as they did not attend the village school. Mrs Thomas, a lady from our village, had clearly been asked to look after them as not all the parents could be there, and she hovered nearby making sure they had everything they wanted to eat. I was lucky enough to be offered a coconut meringue, something I had never had. It was delicious and I mentioned this to Georgina. She asked me if I would like another, but there were no more meringues in sight. Georgina tugged at the hand of the kind lady near them, pointed to me and said imperiously:

'That little girl would like another cake!'

Mrs Thomas sweetly brought over several plates of cakes until we found one which had the desired coconut meringue. I have never forgotten this little episode and I still love coconut meringues!

While a team of ladies cleared the debris from the table, groups of children were sent to the cloakrooms to use the lavatories. The chairs were removed and arranged in rows at the other end of the hall. Photographs were taken, first all the girls and then all the boys, since there were too many to fit into one photo. Then came the best part of the day, the cartoons! A screen was erected and a projector and reel of film set up. The chairs were arranged with an aisle down the middle so that the film was able to be projected clearly.

We did not have a television and I had only been to the cinema once in my life, so watching the cartoons was a particular treat and something which appealed to everyone, even the adults. There were several *Tom & Jerry* cartoons, *Donald Duck,* and *Popeye.*

Then the coaches arrived to take the visiting children back to their own villages and local parents who had not attended would collect their children at the door. Each child was given an apple and an orange to take away with them.

CHAPTER 6

CHRISTMAS EVE AT SUNNYSIDE

John Reeve, together with his elder brother William and sister Lizzie, gave up farming at Union Farm at Dauntsey and retired to Sunnyside, the cottage opposite us, when I was about five years old.

That Christmas Eve, my mother took us to visit in the early evening as she wanted my brothers, who had sweet voices, to sing a few carols for them as Lizzie was unwell and unable to leave the house. John Reeve ushered us into the cosy living room where a bright fire burned in the grate. Lizzie Reeve lay propped up by pillows on a bed at the side of the room, her long grey hair plaited neatly.

John declared his intention of mixing a port and lemon drink for everybody before the carols began. My mother thanked him, saying she and the boys would love some, but that I was too young to have any.

'Ooh, 'twouldn't do the Little Maid any harm,' argued John.

'Oh, no,' she's much too young!' stated my mother.

'But she's not much younger than 'im' said John looking at M.

'She's a year younger.' my mother replied.' He can have some, but she's too young.'

John clearly disagreed with this, but he couldn't argue with my mother. He frowned and turned to poke the fire. 'I'll just make a drink for Lina,' he said, referring to Lizzie.

He busied himself with bottles and glasses and then made some kind of warm drink for Lizzie who had to drink out of an invalid cup which had a small spout. She now needed help holding it steady. While he was preparing this, John kept up a steady stream of conversation with my mother. He distracted my brothers by asking them to decide what carols they were going to sing and they consulted together over their carol sheets.

'Give the Little Maid a drink, John.' Lizzie had heard my mother refuse a drink for me and was anxious about it.

'You have yours first, we'll have one in a minute.' John calmed his frail sister.

He asked my mother to help Lizzie hold her cup while he made up the fire. The instant my mother had turned her back to assist Lizzie, he quickly crossed the room and placed a large glass of port and lemon on the floor by my seat and whispered: 'Get that down you, quick, before yer mum notices,' he smiled at me before turning quickly back to poke the fire. He was careful to keep my mother distracted with the latest village gossip, asking her opinion and keeping her attention focused on himself and the news he was imparting until he was sure I'd drunk the port and lemon. My mother loved to hear what was going on in the village and was totally engrossed in what John was saying.

He glanced quickly in my direction and spotting my empty glass he suppressed a smile as he made drinks for my mother, brothers and himself.

'Has the Little Maid had a drink, John?' enquired Lizzie, looking anxiously in my direction.

'Yes, she's had hers.'

'Oh!' said my mother looking rather flustered.

'She only 'ad a little drop; that won't hurt 'er,' soothed John.

'Oh, alright, it is rather nice,' agreed my mother.

'We always 'ad port and lemon on Christmas Eve, even when we were small children we all 'ad a lit'le drop,' reminisced John. 'I don't suppose there was much port in there, but we all enjoyed it.'

William Reeve came in to join us. He had been visiting their brother and sisters at Yew Tree Farm next door and reported that they were all in good spirits. A few years older than John, he was a quiet, shy man.

Then my brothers stood up and sang two or three carols, their fine, pure voices singing the old familiar tunes. We sat on for a while, enjoying the warmth of the fire and the quiet conversational company of these wise friends before we went home to bed.

CHAPTER 7

FROGSPAWN

'Oh don't go out in those shoes, you'll ruin them! Put your old shoes on,' implored my mother as she turned from washing clothes at the scullery sink. Suds dripped from her hands and glistened for an instant before splattering on the floor in dark splodges. My mother moved to dry her hands on the old blue towel hanging on the hook on the back door.

I looked at my bright new shoes, shining like fresh conkers, and then reluctantly picked up my old ones; scruffy and brown with bare grey patches on each toe where the leather had been worn away. They were concertinaed at the heel where I'd trodden them down and uncomfortable to wear. Reluctantly I tugged at the laces on my new ones and started to prise my right shoe off with the toe of my left one.

'Don't do that! Untie them properly,' instructed my mother sharply. At that point my two older brothers, B and M burst into the room. 'Can we go for a walk?'

'Oh alright, but can you take her with you. I've got all the washing to do,' sighed my mother.

'You'd better behave!' she said, turning to look sternly in my direction.

'M, you wear the wellingtons, I want you to keep your new shoes clean for school.'

M pushed one foot into a wellington where it stuck halfway down. 'They're too small,' he complained.

'Are you sure you can't get them on? enquired my mother, 'They fitted you last term.'

'No, my feet have grown again.'

I looked at the wellington boots hopefully. They were worn and scruffy, but they would allow me to walk in mud and puddles without getting into trouble with my mother. However they were third hand and likely to be smelly. They'd also been standing in the cold, damp scullery all winter and there was a possibility that spiders might have taken up residence. I shuddered.

'Well, I suppose you can wear them.' My mother looked disapprovingly at me. Anything special was usually reserved for my brothers.

'M, try not to get those shoes too dirty, you've got school tomorrow,' reminded my mother. 'B, have you got your old ones on?'

'Yes. Hurry up, Ceri, or we'll go without you,' said B, opening the back door.

'Waaaaait,' I wailed. Thrusting my feet into the boots and grabbing my coat I rushed after my brothers, up the mossy path to the gate, my unbuttoned coat flapping around my knees.

'Come on, quick; the train will be coming in a minute,' shouted M. We rushed down the road, past the old orchard. I paused to admire the ancient bent apple trees, their mossy branches, like the arthritic fingers of the elderly farmers who tended them, stretched towards the sun. I loved the orchard, especially gathering the apples in autumn. The feel and smell of them: *Beauty of Bath, Underleaf, Russet* and *Tom Putt* – each magical name conjuring up a memory to be treasured.

I rushed to catch up with my brothers. Ahead of us was the railway bridge which supported the main line from London to Cardiff and beyond. We stopped underneath it and waited. The bridge had already started to tremble slightly, like a living thing. I pressed my palms tightly over my ears as the trembling became a hum and then a muffled roar. The bridge rattled and shook. My brothers laughed with excitement, their voices echoing strangely under the hollow of the iron girders. Bits of rust showered down on us and a cloud of acrid smoke hung in the air, catching in our throats. Then with a thunderous roar the Great Western express passed over and hurtled onwards. My stomach clenched in fear; the bridge did not seem strong enough to support such a monster. As the deafening roar gradually subsided to a hum again, relief flooded through me that the ordeal was over.

We walked onwards round the bend in the road. It was a bright April day, the young hawthorn greening the hedges and a feeling of spring in the air. We wandered along towards the little hump-backed bridge which spanned the brook. Just before we reached it the verge broadened out and there was a small pond overhung with hawthorn trees.

As we paused to look at it, B gave a cry of delight: 'Frogspawn!'

'Where?' enquired M.

'Over there,' B pointed.

The frogspawn floated in a gelatinous mass about a foot away from the edge of the pond.

'Hey, let's get some,' he exclaimed.

'Oh, no,' said B in a disappointed voice, 'we haven't got a jam jar.'

'Oh,' replied M, 'I'm not going all the way back.'

'Nor am I,' said B. 'What can we carry it in?' B looked around for any stray jars or old paint tins, but people were much tidier then and there was no litter of any kind to be seen, let alone a jam jar.

'Hey, I know!' announced B, 'The wellingtons; we could carry frogspawn home in them!'

'No,' I eyed my brothers warily. I knew them only too well.

'Oh, go on!' B put on his most persuasive voice. 'You're my favourite sister.'

I giggled. 'You only have one sister,' I objected.

'Go on, Ceri,' said M.

'No!' Then sensing that I wasn't going to win I decided that bargaining was my only option. 'What will you give me?'

'You could have some frogspawn of your own. You could keep it in a bucket in the garden,' replied B.

I thought of my wellingtons being filled with clammy frogspawn, 'No!'

'I know,' said M, 'you can have first read of *The Eagle*.'

'Hey,' said B, 'it's my comic, I want to read it first.'

'But we want some frogspawn,' argued M.

'Oh, alright,' said B. 'Come on, give us the wellies.'

I looked dubiously at them. 'Do you *promise?*' I demanded.

'Yes,' said B. I sat down and tugged off my wellingtons. The grass was wet and muddy and I was already beginning to regret my decision.

B was using a stick to manoeuvre a large mass of frogspawn towards one of the wellingtons while M scooped it in. 'We'd better put some water in with it,' he remarked.

'Ugh!' I watched, half fascinated, half horrified as the boots were filled with frogspawn and water.

I shall never forget the journey home, my brothers marching along triumphantly, the sunlight glinting on their fair hair, each clutching a black slimy wellington, while I hobbled along behind, wincing and yelping as I encountered sharp stones or thistles, and trying to pick the smoothest path and keep up at the same time.

My mother wasn't too pleased when she saw what the wellingtons had been used for, but in her eyes my brothers could do no wrong, so after protesting mildly she instructed them to empty the wellingtons immediately into an old bucket.

I hopped about on the cold cement of the scullery in bare feet while I waited for the return of the wellingtons. While I waited I anxiously told my mother about the promise my brothers had made. They often involved me in their schemes with the assurance of some reward, but usually forgot about that as soon as our enterprise was over. The wellingtons were returned to me sodden and squelchy with bits of frogspawn clinging to their sides. Despite this my mother insisted that if I wanted to go into the garden to see the frogspawn I would have to put them back on again and it was no use wearing socks as they would only get wet and have to be washed.

Gingerly, and with many exclamations of horror and disgust, I stepped into the wellingtons and squelched into the garden to admire the frogspawn.

However, when *The Eagle* was delivered that week, my mother insisted that I have first read, ignoring my brothers' protests that we hadn't shaken hands on the deal.

Quite right too! Putting my bare feet back into those wellingtons was like putting my feet into a dish of ice cold jelly. I still shudder at the memory.

CHAPTER 8

LITTLE SOMERFORD SCHOOL

Little Somerford school was a typical Victorian village school with its big main schoolroom and church style windows carefully positioned so that no child seated at their desk could see anything outside apart from sky. A door opened into a smaller classroom where the infants were taught. Lavatories and a small cloakroom had been built on in recent years. The building was heated by two enormous pot-bellied stoves, one in each classroom. They were guarded by iron railings and fuelled by coke. If your desk happened to be nearby you were cosy and warm, but anyone seated further away had to get used to cooler temperatures and cold draughts.

Mrs Perks was the headmistress at Little Somerford school. She came to Great Somerford during the Second World War when she accompanied Jewish refugees from London. She liked the area and stayed on after the war and in the early 1950s became headmistress at Little Somerford School. Previously the teacher was Mr Warren, who had lived at Sunnyside opposite our house.

Mrs Perks was appointed when the Warrens moved to Wales. Mr Perks sadly died a few years after she became headmistress.

Mrs Perks's house was next door to the school. It was a very pretty cottage of Cotswold stone, set in a large and beautiful garden which had a paved area in front of the house, together with a lawn and herbaceous border, and an extensive vegetable patch at the back. Flowering cherry trees adorned the lawn and a gravelled drive at the side of the garden led to a garage at one end of the house. Mrs Perks was a keen gardener and the garden was well tended.

When our eighty year old neighbour was at the school, there were over a hundred children. Now there were about thirty-seven in the whole school and numbers were a constant worry as the headmistress was anxious to keep two teachers there. As soon as a child was four and three quarters their parents were asked to send them to school.

First there was the interview with Mrs Perks, known behind her back by the older children as 'Fanny.' I remember my mother reminding me to answer any questions politely. My hair was combed and I was made to wear a clean cardigan before we walked down to the lovely stone cottage next to the school. Mrs Perks was a plump lady with a florid complexion and short grey hair. She was very cultured and accomplished and later inspired my love of poetry. She was also extremely good at needlework of all kinds.

I remember her asking my mother if I could count to

ten, and whether I could tie my shoelaces. I could count, but not tie my shoelaces yet. I would have to learn this quickly as school started the following week. It was also decided that I should be called Ceri as nobody would be able to pronounce Ceridwen.

There were a good number of children in the infants' room that autumn – twenty in all. One person had to be moved up into the big room to even out the numbers.

We were divided by age into three groups named Teddy House, Seven Springs and Hut House.

These were named because Eileen had her teddy on the first day, the 'Seven Springs' were meant to be the seven springs of wisdom, and the 'Hut House' group were making huts in their topic work.

There were three others in Teddy House: Angela Gutteridge, a bright little girl; Pauline Parfitt, a pretty girl who was beautifully dressed by her mother; Eileen Parsloe, who had brown bobbed hair and a delicate complexion; and myself, a quiet, shy child with light brown hair and green eyes. The highlight of my day was the little third of a pint bottle of milk which we each had at break time. We spent most of the morning drawing, at least Pauline, Angela and I did. Eileen spent the whole morning in floods of tears in spite of having her teddy to keep her company. At lunch time she had to be taken home, but as she lived next door to the school this was just a matter of handing her over the fence to her mother! However, the next day, she came in smiling and settled happily into school life.

Our teacher was Miss Downey, a kind but scatterbrained lady with frizzy dark hair.

She was especially fond of her nephew, Graham, who lived in Somerset, but who was often held up to us as a shining example of someone who excelled at whatever it was that we couldn't do. He was referred to as 'The Somerset Boy'. My brother M was thought to be similar in some respects; they shared a birthday and were both left-handed, and since he had beautiful blond hair and blue eyes, he quickly became her favourite within the class. I really preferred being left-handed, but I wasn't allowed to be. Only special people were left-handed!

Eventually, as the term went on, a little more time was made for our group and we learned to write the alphabet and started to read. We worked our way through *Janet and John* and then *The Beacon Readers*. Our mornings were spent doing arithmetic, reading and writing. In the afternoons we did art or craft.

On one occasion just after I had started school, we had been painting, and after wiping over the oil cloth that was used to protect my desk with a wet rag, I asked Miss Downey where it had to go. She was busy hearing one of the older children read and didn't have any time to spare for me.

'Oh, just throw it over the fire,' she replied distractedly. Mindful of my mother's instructions to do exactly as I was told, I threw the cloth over the stove. There was a great hiss of steam as the wet cloth came into contact with the hot metal. I watched, mesmerized, as the cloth started to writhe and shrivel like a live thing. It disintegrated into bits and a foul smell filled the air. Mrs

Perks rushed in to see what all the noise was about and sent everyone else outside for an early playtime.

'Why on earth did you put that cloth on the fire?' she asked me.

'Miss Downey said,' I replied.

'I didn't mean you to throw it on the fire,' retorted Miss Downey.

'You *said,'* I insisted. 'You *said* just throw it over the fire!'

Mrs Perks groaned loudly and looked accusingly at Miss Downey. There was nothing she could say because she knew Miss Downey had really said that, even though I should not have taken it literally. I was in disgrace for the rest of the day and decided I had to be careful about doing what I was told in future.

CHAPTER 9

HARVEST FESTIVAL

One of the most important happenings of the term was Harvest Festival. We were all marched down the road to the church to decorate it. Sheaves of wheat had been donated by a kind local farmer and we were meant to tie bunches of this on the ends of the pews. We pounced on the wheat with joy, nearly driving Miss Downey to distraction as some of the naughtier children tried to stuff it down their neighbour's neck and chaos ensued. Stalks of wheat were spread haphazardly all up the nave and trodden into the red carpet.

Eventually, after dire threats of missed playtimes, order was restored and uneven bunches were gathered enthusiastically and tied in lop-sided, drooping bundles to the pew ends. At last it was done and we were herded into line and hurried back to school for lunch before the great occasion.

After lunch we were assembled again and marched in great excitement back to the church. This time parents would be joining us for the service and watching their offspring proudly as they carried fruit and giant marrows up to the altar steps.

I was rather puzzled when we were directed to our pew. I was first in the line and sat down next to a tall, sturdy lady in an olive green coat. She had dark, wavy hair pinned neatly at shoulder length beneath a small hat. She also happened to be eating chocolates out of a large white paper bag in her lap. At the age of four and three-quarters I was not familiar with church etiquette, but even at the time this seemed strange to me. Suddenly, the lady vanished just as the rest of my group were being squeezed into the pew.

'You can't sit there,' I told them, 'that's a lady's place.'

At that moment I saw her again, but the others evidently could not, and sat down regardless. I stared in surprise, but the lady had gone. I tried to explain it to my mother later, but naturally she did not believe me. Years later, when I was about fourteen an elderly neighbour told us about Miss Preddy, who used to keep the village sweet shop. From her description I recognised the lady I saw in church, though at the time I saw her she had been dead for some years!

CHAPTER 10

LESSONS

After two years in the infants class I was moved up into the big room, together with Eileen, Angela and Pauline. We were joined by a new girl called Christine Cuss who lived at Cleverton, a little hamlet just beyond Somerford.

The school day began with a hymn and a prayer. Mrs Perks played the piano for morning assembly. *Morning Has Broken, When a Knight Won His Spurs* or *He Who Would Valiant Be* were favourite hymns followed by a Bible story. In the mornings we did Maths and English.

To begin with we always worked in grammar books, but as we grew older we learned to write essays, and spellings were set for homework. We were introduced to a wide range of poetry including poets such as John Clare, Walter de la Mare and Rupert Brooke, and a love of poetry has remained with me.

On Mondays we had a wonderful radio programme called '*Singing Together*' for which we had a booklet of songs to learn each term. These were English, Irish, Scottish or Welsh folk songs, and carols during the autumn term. Physical Education consisted of playing with hoops, balls, bean bags and skipping ropes as the playground was not large. After a few terms the school acquired some mats for P.E. which were dragged out from their shed in dry weather and used to practise forward rolls, handstands and cartwheels. In the summer we occasionally played rounders in a nearby field. Our plimsolls were known as *daps* and we had a dap-bag, made by our mothers, which was a drawstring bag made of cloth to keep them in.

I learned to do joined up writing using the Marion Richardson method. This method of teaching handwriting involved children copying rows of letter patterns from a book, such as rows of letter *ffffff* or *gggggggggg*. Each desk had a hole in the top corners where a china inkwell was fitted and these were filled with ink when our writing was deemed good enough for us to be issued with a pen. These were dipping pens, just a wooden handle into which a pen nib was slotted and we had to dip the pens regularly into the inkwell as we wrote. This involved some skill in order to avoid blotches of ink on one's work.

In the afternoons we did art or craft. We only had powder paints in primary colours and had to mix all these together to make a sludgy black. On one occasion I painted my paper black all over. When Mrs Perks asked me why I had done this, I replied: 'It's night! Night's black!' and was immediately smacked on the back of my leg.

Sometimes we made puppets out of papier mâché.

A face and neck and back of head were made separately out of plasticene and then coated with Vaseline to ensure that the finished puppet could be prised away when it was finished. Strips of newspaper were then glued across the plasticene until seven or eight layers had been completed. This was left to dry. Then the plasticine was removed and the two pieces trimmed and stuck together to make the head of the puppet.

We had a lot of fun painting the faces and making costumes for them. Then in groups we wrote and performed puppet plays. If these were any good, the infants were sometimes invited into the Big Room to watch a performance. While we worked on our puppets, Mrs Perks would make the most beautiful dolls out of stuffed felt. Sometimes these were raffled at the Christmas Bazaar.

We made gingham aprons embroidered with rows of cross stitches, needle cases and felt pictures sewn onto a cloth background. I also made a beautiful handkerchief case for my mother. Despite my winning prizes at the Somerford Show with some of these, Mrs Perks declared me to be the most impractical child she had ever encountered!

Once a week we heard a nature programme on the radio which involved two characters called '*Mr Collins and Tony.*' In this programme Mr Collins would tell the boy, Tony, about a different animal or bird and Tony would ask questions about it. Each week we learned about the life of a different animal such as a squirrel, or a frog. We were tested afterwards with ten questions. The younger children had easier questions than the older ones and at the end of term the top person in each group won a prize. We also had Music and Movement for which we cleared the desks and chairs to one side so that we could stomp around to the music. *Morning* and *The Hall of the Mountain King* by Grieg often seemed to feature.

School dinners were delivered in heated canisters by a lovely lady called Dora Spackman who drove the van. One winter's day the van skidded into a ditch and our dinner did not arrive. I and my friend Christine were sent to the shop for a loaf of bread, a packet of butter and a big bag of sweets and we enjoyed this makeshift meal as much as a school dinner. We later heard rumours of a local ditch running with school gravy!

On rare occasions we were allowed to go to Mrs Perks's schoolhouse next door to watch a geography programme on television. I was more interested in Mrs Perks's cat. Bola (short for Bolingbroke) was a disdainful ball of white fluff, who generally ignored all efforts to attract his attention. Despite several overtures of friendship from us, Bola usually remained aloof and sulked under a chair until we had departed.

At playtime we all rushed into the playground. In spring we played skipping games or marbles. There were seasonal games such as conkers in the autumn, followed by chain tag with the poor child on the end of the line hurtling round so fast their feet barely touched the ground. In snowy weather we made lethal slides which would never be allowed these days, often begging Mrs Scott, who washed the dinner things, for jugs of hot water to make the slide even more slippery, but accidents were rare. On one occasion I fell on my nose in the playground and broke it badly. I was just told to sit quietly, though afterwards Mrs Perks said that she had better enter it in the school log. By the time I got home my nose was extremely swollen, but although my mother said it was probably broken, she just told me not to make a fuss!

Our school day usually ended with a story or silent reading, followed by a prayer at home time, but once a week we had 'Speeches' where we had to stand in front of the class and talk about something which interested us. I never won prizes for speeches. For one thing I was too shy, and for another I did not get help at home with my speech, whereas some children did.

Our standard of reading was extremely high. Little Somerford school had a good Eleven Plus pass rate and a number of children came from Great Somerford in order to have a better chance of getting to Malmesbury Grammar School. By the age of seven I had a reading age of fourteen, but this was also partly because I read a great deal at home. We won one of ten televisions given by Wiltshire County Council to the schools with the highest standard of reading in the county.

In warm weather we had occasional nature walks. One walk was to Kingsmead Mill where Mr Fry opened the wheelhouse and showed us the great water wheel, dank and dripping above the roar of the millrace. We had a trip to Kingsmead level crossing where Bill Archard explained his job as crossing keeper and how the railway line had been altered to go to our village station rather than Great Somerford. On other occasions we collected leaves or flowers for the nature table.

As the dreaded Eleven Plus exam drew nearer we had extra sums to do before school started. After the English exam, we all discovered that we had written about The Tiger. We were given the afternoon off and the rector, Mr Lutley, took us back to the rectory at Great Somerford and gave us tea and cakes and showed us the tiger skin rug in his drawing room.

Village teachers such as Mrs Perks at Little Somerford did a wonderful job. Children learned the basics: reading, writing and arithmetic. The standard of spelling and writing was generally above average and the times tables up to twelve were learned by heart. Children had a wide knowledge of English folk songs, the skills of sewing and other crafts, they could identify most of the flowers and wild animals around them and were ready to learn when they moved on to their senior schools.

A few years after I left it, the village school was closed, much to the disappointment of the villagers who all had fond memories of it. The school was converted into a house and several new houses were built on the playground. Children from the village were sent to Great Somerford school.

CHAPTER 11

THE GARAGE

'Could you get some paraffin for me?' asked my mother, eyeing me for any sign of resistance.

'Why can't the boys go?' I countered.

'M went last time and B has homework to do,' replied my mother.

'But it's too heavy for me.'

'You'll have to go down twice and get half a gallon each time; it won't take very long,' stated my mother.

'It's dark, I don't like the dark,' I objected.

'Baby!' sneered M, poking his tongue out at me behind our mother's back.

I scowled at him in return.

'You can take the torch. Hurry up, or they'll be closed and then the heater will go out and we'll be cold,' repeated my mother firmly.

Sighing, I shrugged on my coat and took the dirty white plastic container from her, and with a heavy torch in my other hand I trotted out. There was no street lighting then and the darkness was all enveloping until my eyes adjusted to it. My breath clouded in the cold air and high above me stars glittered; there was going to be a frost tonight.

The thick garden hedges soon obscured the light from the living room window and the trees in the little orchard next door loomed up against the dark, their twiggy branches reaching out for me. I stumbled over the uneven grass, nearly dropping my torch in shock when an animal in Butcher's Orchard opposite rustled against the hedge. I hurried along the verge until I reached Street Farm. This was the worst part of the journey as the open cart sheds by the gateway were black, cavernous mouths where monsters might lurk.

I shuddered and hurried past, my heart thumping in my chest. Here I was able to turn onto the tarmac footpath which ran past Street Farmhouse and the paddock next to it and on round the corner opposite our school. The playground, which had been full of noisy children earlier in the day, was now still and eerily quiet.

I walked on past the old Chapel Cottage, past the farm drive and Manor Farm itself. The wall obscured the lower windows, but there was a light on in an upper window. I imagined somebody dressing to go out. Then another field and the large garden of Somerford House, but I could see the lighted windows from the houses opposite, next to the church, and this cheered me. I soon stepped off the footpath and walked into the garage.

George Higgs, who ran the garage with his brother Alfie, was a tall, slim, silver-haired man who always wore a long brown coat to serve customers, and whistled cheerfully to himself as he went about his work. Alfie was younger and had dark brown crinkly hair and a burlier build. He was usually in the old forge building repairing cars and sometimes emerged if George was out, wiping his hands on an oily rag. I peered around the open doorway of the large shed to see if George was there. Its walls were of corrugated metal sheets painted gunmetal grey. Inside, my footsteps echoed hollowly in the large space and there was a pungent odour of oil, rubber and paraffin which made me wrinkle my nose in disgust.

'Hello, dear,' said George. 'You're a bit young to be out in the dark. How old are you?'

'Six,' I replied.

'You're one of the Vyners aren't you? What's your name?'

'Yes,' I nodded, 'I'm Ceri.'

'Where are your brothers? They should be getting the paraffin, not you.' There was a look of concern on his face.

'It was my turn,' I stated.

'Humph!' he snorted. 'How much paraffin d'you want? I don't suppose you can carry a gallon.'

'Half a gallon, please, and I'll have to come down again for the rest.'

There was another humph of disapproval and I looked up anxiously.

'I normally only sell it by the gallon!'

George thought for a moment, glanced at my pleading face, and then sighed and went to get the paraffin.

I looked around curiously. A few bicycle tyres, inner

tubes, pumps and puncture repair kits were displayed for sale on one wall near a cash machine which stood on a high counter. A box of Ever-Ready batteries sat on the shelf behind, along with a large cardboard box containing bags of Smiths Crisps. Each packet had salt in a twist of blue waxed paper and any purchaser had the ritual of digging down carefully inside the packet to find it and sprinkling the salt on the crisps before enjoying them. The crisps cost sixpence.

I tried to hold my breath against the strong smell of paraffin, at the same time marvelling at the beautiful violet colour of the fuel as I watched George carefully filling our container from a large five gallon drum. He removed the funnel and screwed the caps on both containers before wiping his hands and taking payment. Then he picked up my plastic fuel can and kindly carried it out across the forecourt for me and reminded me to be careful on the road. I gulped in the fresh air with a sigh of relief before thanking George and promising to come straight back for the other half gallon. I picked up the heavy load, thrusting my other arm out to balance myself against the weight of it before starting the slow trudge back. As I did so, I turned back for an instant to glance up at the three large Shell petrol pumps with their circular tops. Silhouetted against the glow of light from the open shed door, they gave the impression that three very large people were standing in a row.

CHAPTER 12

GAMES

Many of our games were seasonal. In spring we played skipping, leapfrog and marbles in the school playground. There were various skipping rhymes sung by the girls, such as *Green Gravel* and *Teddy Bear, Teddy Bear* which was a rhyme describing actions which the skipper had to perform or mime without tripping up.

Teddy bear, teddy bear touch the ground,
Teddy bear, teddy bear turn right round.
Teddy bear, teddy bear, show your shoe,
Teddy bear, teddy bear that will do.
Teddy bear, teddy bear go upstairs,
Teddy bear, teddy bear say your prayers,
Teddy bear, teddy bear turn out the light,
Teddy bear, teddy bear say goodnight.

The actions became progressively more difficult until the skipper stumbled and had to take their turn at holding the rope. The *Green Gravel* song was popular with the older girls as it enabled them to embarrass their peers.

Green Gravel, Green Gravel, your age is
(number) years.
I'll tell your mother you've been seen
Kissing (boy's name) on the green!
How many kisses did he give?

Here the skipping became faster and faster and each skip was counted aloud as a kiss! The skipper soon tripped up and had to swap places with someone else and the rhyme began again.

We also played chain tag, each caught person linking hands with the searcher until a long line of children were hurtling around the playground at top speed. Another tag game involved the caught person standing still with their arms outstretched so that someone on the loose could touch them and thus free them again.

We all had collections of marbles including a large ally which was much prized. During the summer we sometimes played rounders in Colonel Brassey's field halfway up The Hill. Jumpers were used to mark the posts. Usually one or more of the Porter or Parsloe girls would join us.

At home we played many games of cricket on the front lawn, using a homemade bat and a tennis ball. The large staddle stone near the house, known by us all as *The Saddle Stone,* was our stump. Any ball hit over the hedge into the orchard was a six, but the game had to be paused while the ball was retrieved. M was very keen on cricket, but since England generally won in those days I always had to represent Pakistan!

In the autumn term conkers were very popular during September. There was one huge chestnut tree over the fields beyond the railway bridge on the Dauntsey Road and we always had an expedition there to gather conkers. Various methods were used to harden up the conkers: soaking in vinegar, baking them in the oven or coating them with varnish. Breaks and lunch times were spent playing Conkers or watching other children play and wild boasts were made about the durability of our chosen conkers. Then, suddenly, the conker craze was over and, as the weather became colder, tag became the popular game again.

B made a trolley out of a set of pram wheels and the pram handle was fixed to the front axle so that it could be used to steer the vehicle as well as pull it along. For years the trolley was used to carry shopping from the bus stop at the top of The Hill or to haul a sack of potatoes or a bale of hay (for the rabbits) from the farm over the road.

We made tree houses and camps in pollarded ash and willow trees, and as the youngest I was always sent over to Yew Tree Farm to beg for baler twine. Ernest Reeve who farmed there, was very generous and gave me a whole armful of twine when I explained that we wanted to make a rope ladder.

One summer M borrowed a tent from a friend and we slept out in it in the garden. We did not have a ground sheet, so we had to make one. M asked kind Mr Gawthropp for some plastic fertiliser sacks which we carefully cut open, washed, dried and stapled together. These worked very well.

When I was ten there was a craze for stilts. My parents could not afford to buy me any so I asked John Reeve who lived opposite if he had any sticks in his woodpile which I could use. Carefully he moved every branch in the large pile and after examining each one he chose the two most suitable sticks and trimmed them up neatly with a billhook. This was done in such a clever way that a part of a side branch was cut so that it could be used to support a step for my feet. A small piece of wood was nailed in place to make the step and the ends measured and sawn to make them level. I was so grateful for his kindness. The stilts were great fun and after much practice I was able to walk all around the village on them, even walking all the way up The Hill to Wendy Barnes's house right at the top, a good, steep half mile from our house.

When I was about nine a Brownie pack was set up in Little Somerford. It was run by two lovely ladies, Mrs Parsloe from Little Somerford and Mrs Elmer who lived at Great Somerford. Several girls came from Great Somerford and we met once a week in Little Somerford School. There were eleven of us in all and we were in three teams, Swallows, Blue Tits and Kingfishers. I was a Kingfisher.

We learnt many useful things such as basic first aid, how to turn our ties into an emergency sling and how to fold the triangular piece of material back into a tie again. We sent messages to each other using semaphore flags in the school playground. We worked for individual badges such as Housekeeper badge for which we had to learn to iron a shirt, make a bed and lay a table. We all took our Cook's badge and for that we had to cook a meal, which included making custard. I went to the local antiquarian bookseller, Richard Hatchwell, to be tested for my Reader's badge and the Hatchwells also allowed me to bath three of their children and get them ready for bed for my Childcare badge. This was so successful that they later employed me as a babysitter throughout my teenage years.

We learned how to tie several useful knots and practised memory training games such as *Kim's Game* and *I Packed my Trunk.*

Once we were too old for Brownies, several of us became Girl Guides and I joined the Great Somerford pack, also run by Mrs Elmer. Meetings were held in Great Somerford School There we learned knots, more first aid and how to lay and light a campfire. We cooked sausages and Dampers (a kind of pastry wound around a stick) on a campfire in a nearby field and then had a sing song after the food was eaten. We played tracking games around Great Somerford and generally had a good time.

CHAPTER 13

STREET FARM

'Let'n went!' exclaimed Malcolm Stoneham as the piglet, uttering a shrill squeal, dived between our legs as we tried for the tenth time to round it up and return it to all the others in the sty.

Nigel Maidment, whose parents owned Street Farm, had enlisted our help to try to catch it and he and Malcolm, a neighbour's son, and my brother M and I had spent over half an hour frantically trying to corner the beast in the farmyard. Escaped animals were a feature of our lives then and we were often startled by a loud knock at our cottage door and a plea to help round up loose animals.

I frequently spent time at Street Farm, a handsome farmhouse, painted white and roofed with Cotswold tiles, surrounded by fields right in the centre of the village. It was owned by John and Audrey Maidment whose younger son, Nigel was the same age as my brother M.

On one occasion the pigs in the Little Orchard between Street Farm and our garden, broke through the hedge and rooted up all my mother's cabbage and bean plants. We eventually herded them back through the gap, but not before the vegetable crops were decimated. My father attempted to block the gap in the hedge and complained bitterly to Mr Maidment, who arrived soon after, that it was the fourth time that week that the pigs had broken through and he really needed to repair the fence.

'Yer a haaard man, Mr Vyner!' came the reply, much to our amusement. My brothers later used this expression whenever they were told off.

We often walked down the dirt track and under the railway arch to the further fields to bring the cows up to the farm to be milked. These were mostly black and white shorthorn cattle, but with one Jersey cow whose milk would give extra creaminess to the milk so that they could get more money for it.

The cows had names and they all knew their places in the cowshed and would wait patiently in their stalls to be chained up. We helped to put out a few pieces of cow cake in each metal feed dish attached to the wall of their stall, while the hum of the milking machine started up. We watched as udders were washed and the milking machine attached so that its rhythmic movement caused the milk to flow smoothly down the rubber tubes and into the churns. The air smelled of cows and milk and cow dung, but strangely enough this was not unpleasant. Sometimes there was a cow which had to be milked by hand and Mr Maidment would squat on a short three-legged stool, leaning his head into the cow's flank, singing a snatch of the latest pop song as he milked, and holding the metal bucket between his knees in case the cow kicked it. It was a very contented scene.

There was the gentle humming of the milking machine, the low mooing and occasional snort of cows, the intermittent splashing noises as the animals relieved themselves and the rasp of the stiff brush on the concrete floor of the cowshed as the manure was swept away. Once the milking was over the cows were unchained and ambled back down to their field in their slow and stately way, the three of us following behind to close their field gate.

I particularly remember one sweet natured Jersey cow called Nicey because Nigel, M and I had been discussing the possibility of riding cows and the boys, unwilling to experiment themselves, hoisted me up onto Nicey's back. The ride was extremely uncomfortable as Nicey's backbone was exceptionally bony and the track rutted and uneven. There was nothing to hold on to, and I slid off after a short time.

Sometimes Mr Maidment gave us a ride down on his grey Ford tractor, all three of us bouncing up and down as the tractor lurched over the ruts in the track. The deafening growl of the engine, the acrid stink of the exhaust in our nostrils and the certain knowledge of our mother's deep disapproval only added to the excitement.

In winter, along with a few other village children, we played *Blind Man's Buff* in one of the small sheds where dry pig swill mix and cow cake were stored in paper sacks. There was the added horror of the blindfolded person reaching out to catch someone, but instead thrusting their hands into one of the huge dusty cobwebs complete with large black spiders which adorned the upper walls.

The farmyard was a creepy place after dark and we played a kind of hide and seek game called *Jack, Jack, Show Your Light* whereby two people went to hide and two searched for them. When almost discovered, the hiders had to shine a torch away from themselves to try to deceive the searchers and when the hiders were found, the searchers had to call out *'Jack, Jack, show your light'*, whereupon the hiders had to shine the torch on themselves and pull a hideous face at the children who had discovered them.

Once I picked up a hen in one of the barns and later found myself crawling with horrible black chicken mites. I had to strip off in our scullery and my clothes had to be dunked in several buckets of boiling water to kill the creatures. Then I had to have a strip wash and have my hair washed about five times in warm water and combed through until all the mites had been dealt with. I kept clear of hens after that!

We were lucky to really get to know the animals: pigs, cows and occasionally a few sheep were kept as well as hens, ducks and geese. We helped to collect the hens' eggs and admired the yellow goslings as we moved their pen to a new patch of grass in the paddock. We were able to watch at first hand the sheep shearing, helping to hold the animals down as they were sheared. Afterwards they would rise hastily to their feet and shamble off with puzzled expressions as they felt the spring air on their bare skin. The warm fleeces felt slightly oily to the touch as they were rolled up and bundled into sacks.

Haymaking was always a favourite time. The sweet meadow grass, once a mass of wildflowers and waving grass stems, was cut into long swathes. Then, when these had been dried on one side, the hay was turned over to dry the underside before it could be gathered into stooks. These consisted of a large armful of hay tied around the middle with binder twine. Then three would be propped up together to dry out a bit more before being gathered in. At first an old binding machine was used and I remember playing among the stooks in Butcher's Orchard, now covered by the Vale Leaze housing estate. Within a few years all the farmers used the modern bailers which packed the hay into compact rectangular bales which were much easier to stack. These were stored in hay barns and not made into ricks like the stooks. The smell of hay was intoxicating and to walk in the hay barn in winter was to bring back sweet summer in one waft of air.

Sometimes we played tracking over the fields, using sticks and chalk to mark our direction, 'home' being a bale of hay in the farm yard. Children had so much more freedom then; our only rules were never to walk over growing crops, be sensible around animals and not to leave gates open. We could be out until teatime or bedtime if it was summer.

CHAPTER 14

LIFE IN THE GARDEN

I used to run out on to the dewy grass and turn cartwheels for pure joy. The beauty of the front garden was entrancing, and I loved it even as a very small child. It was not over-tidied or regimented like so many gardens today.

From early January, snowdrops spread freely all around its edges and lasted for weeks. Then came forsythia so old it was a small tree, soon followed by apple blossom, hawthorn, purple and white lilac, and laburnum.

The grass, ankle deep and studded with white clover and daisies, was a rich green, while the delicate lavender-coloured lady's smock and the occasional cowslip grew in the damper area under the forsythia's shadow. Two triangular flower beds in the far part of the lawn were a mass of purple vetch, white daisies and sweet rocket in summer, and later, Michaelmas daisies attracted the last of the butterflies.

Wild arum, known to us as cuckoo pint, and the purple flowers that heralded the silvery seed covers of honesty grew in the thick hedges. The larger grassed area next to the house was used as our cricket pitch. At one side of the lawn stood a large and ancient staddle stone. One of the pigs from Street Farm broke into the garden and used the staddle stone as a scratching post, knocking the top off. It was such a weight that my father and three strong village men only just managed to lift it back.

A huge round box bush growing almost against the hedge was used as a den when we were small and was perfect for hiding beneath, being dry and dusty and enabling us to peer out whilst remaining hidden ourselves. A clump of about ten lilac trees at the very end of the garden was known as *The Forest.* In spring that area was carpeted in a great mass of snowdrops; otherwise it provided a plentiful supply of moss for miniature gardens.

Next to the house was a crazy paving path where columbines, stonecrop and everlasting sweet peas grew in profusion, and the lawn was bordered by a narrow flower bed overflowing with lavender bushes, sweet arabis and aubretia. Another flower bed at the far side of the lawn, near the orchard hedge, was carpeted with white bells during May and later, golden rod and Japanese anemones grew freely. A hawthorn hedge separated it from the orchard beyond.

We had to help our mother with gardening from an early age, first holding vegetable seeds such as peas and handing them a few at a time to her as she planted the rows, or helping to pour out cups of water over delicate lettuce or cabbage seedlings. I was encouraged to weed the crazy paving path, while my brothers, as soon as they were strong enough, were persuaded to help cut the hedges or the grass. My other jobs were picking and shelling peas and broad beans, trimming runner beans, picking soft fruit for pies and crumbles, or gathering apples. There was always something to do.

In those days the dawn chorus was deafening and I was often woken up by birdsong. Blackbirds, thrushes and robins were happy to bring up their nestlings behind the thick screen of privet and hawthorn which surrounded the garden. We would peer at the nests, but were careful not to touch the eggs or nestlings within. Green woodpeckers and starlings flew in to feast on the ants on the front lawn. Blue tits, coal tits and great tits flitted round the garden looking for insects and little owls and barn owls nested in the orchard next door.

On one occasion, taking some newspapers to the old stable which served as a wood and rubbish store, I heard a loud hissing sound coming from the other side of the wall. Peering through a convenient crack in the stone I saw a barn owl family on the edge of the stable loft which faced the orchard. An adult owl arrived with a mouse for the three downy-feathered nestlings who perched blinking in the half light. I watched entranced as the parent owl tore the mouse into bite sized pieces and fed them to its offspring.

Hedgehogs rooted around at night. Once we discovered an orphaned hedgehog hoglet. The poor little creature was so small its spines were still pink and soft. It was too small to take the teaspoon of milk we offered and we feared it would die. As a last resort we placed it in the manger in the barn next door, where our tabby cat was nursing a litter of kittens. Caramel, being a motherly cat, fed and cared for the little hedgehog for two weeks, then it disappeared! Although we never saw it again, there were always hedgehogs in the garden after that, so we like to think it survived.

On several occasions Caramel and her kittens had to be moved from the manger to a safer place if the hayloft was occupied by the owls.

Butterflies were numerous: tortoiseshells, red admirals, peacocks, orange tips and meadow browns fluttered around the flowers and my mother waged a constant war with the cabbage whites which threatened to decimate her cabbage and broccoli plants.

The beautiful pinky-red cinnabar moths lived in the hypericum plants by the house wall. We kept hairy caterpillars in jam jars, feeding them on leaves.

Snails were plentiful and when we were small, we used to have snail races up the kitchen door. A toad lived under the old stone sink near the gate and crawled out from time to time looking for food. Once, a very large green grasshopper, the size of my fist was found on the lawn. Pipistrelle bats lived in the attic and flew out at dusk, uttering high pitched squeaks as they searched for insects. The squeaks were clearly audible to us children although my mother could not hear them.

We looked forward to April when we would hear the cuckoo again. Once they arrived, they were never far away; we heard them with the dawn chorus at 4.30am and they called constantly until dusk. On one memorable occasion, I was helping my parents in the kitchen garden when we heard a cacophony of cuckooing. 'Stand still,' ordered my father, and over the house flew five cuckoos, all calling loudly. They perched briefly in the Victoria plum tree, and cuckooed loudly for two or three minutes before taking off again and their beautiful notes gradually became fainter, before fading away.

In summer we kept a careful eye on ripening strawberries as blackbirds and thrushes enjoyed them as much as we did. We did not have netting, so jam jars were placed over the most luscious looking fruits and these not only kept slugs away, but acted like mini-greenhouses too. We had a succession of fruits: gooseberries, black, red and white currants, raspberries, strawberries, rhubarb, purple plums, Victoria plums, damsons, pears, quinces and apples. In September, when we got home from school, we would rush out to forage in the garden. One pear tree produced a large crop of small, sweet fruits, which would not keep, so we were allowed to eat these. My brothers would throw sticks up to knock down the ripest fruit. These pears were very juicy and much sought after, not only by us, but by swarms of wasps so we had to pick up windfalls with caution. The other pear tree was a Williams pear, with fruits much prized by our parents so we were forbidden to help ourselves to these. There was a plum tree in the 'forest' at the end of the front garden whose fruits we were allowed to eat. My mother used to make delicious jam from the damsons.

We grew most of our vegetables. One plot contained

first early and main crop potatoes and also onions. Another patch contained peas, broad and runner beans, cabbages, spring greens, cauliflowers, lettuces, and sprouts. The vegetables were rotated annually so that crops were not grown on the same plot as the previous year. Marrows were grown in a small hot bed at the end of the strawberry patch. A few radishes and spring onions were grown wherever they could be fitted in. There was a large rosemary bush by the gate, and mint, sage, chives parsley and thyme grew at one end of a vegetable patch. From May onwards there was always something to harvest and more things to plant. Any glut of fruit or vegetables was passed on to neighbours and we all had to do our bit: picking fruit, watering plants, digging up potatoes for lunch, cutting a lettuce for tea. Later in the year there would be apples to be picked and sorted and the best ones wrapped in newspaper and stored over the winter.

My brothers and I were expected to help with the garden bonfire which was a weekly event between March and November. There were so many plants to be cut down or cut back. Anything not suitable for compost was put on the bonfire. We were encouraged to bring seemingly endless armfuls of greenery from trimmed shrubs or hedges to the bonfire which sputtered and smoked as it encountered the green sap. Then it would splutter into life, the pungent smell filling the air as the bonfire started to crackle and burn. Warm summer evenings were full of the nostalgic, slightly acrid smell of burning vegetation, which clung to our clothes and mingled with the scent of honeysuckle and jasmine as it drifted skywards. Even now, many years later, the scent of a garden bonfire takes me back to my childhood. Occasionally we were allowed to create our own small fire in a specially dug hole in a spare section of a vegetable patch. Once this got going we would bake potatoes or apples on the embers. The potatoes were usually half raw on the inside and charred on the outside, but we ate them anyway.

My mother was the gardener working for hours on long summer evenings, so that we had to put ourselves reluctantly to bed. It was hard to sleep when the garden was so enticing and the scent of flowers and cut grass filled the summery dusk.

CHAPTER 15

THE SHOP

The village shop was on the side of the Three Crowns public house at the bottom of the Hill not far from Little Somerford Corner. It was run by Bert and Joyce Carroll. Bert ran the pub and Joyce sometimes served in the shop. She was a tall, cheerful lady with dark brown curls, dark eyes and a wide smile which revealed large teeth.

Any enquiry about the quality or taste of anything edible in the shop occasioned the same answer: 'Our Bert 'ad it fer 'is supper larst night, an 'e said it wuz delicious!'

Often, however, customers were served by Dot, a prim, pink-faced lady with fine white hair which was so tightly permed you could see acres of pink scalp between the curls. Dot lived in Lea, the next village on the Malmesbury Road. Her best friend in the village was Mrs Parsloe who did most of her shopping in the village shop in order to exchange gossip with Dot.

Twice a week Mrs Parsloe, a short woman with iron grey curls and a neat figure, took up her position, leaning on the shop counter with one hand, the other clutching a long shopping list. Sometimes she perched on a high stool next to the counter, ready for a long natter.

One could be held up for hours while they gossiped and I was several times in trouble with my parents, having been sent to the shop for an urgent item, only to be delayed by Mrs Parsloe's endless talk.

'Dear oh dear, would you believe it, Dot?' murmured Mrs Parsloe, shaking her curls incredulously.

'Well, when 'e come in 'ere larst week, I thought 'e din't look too good.'

'Ooh, I say!' Mrs Parsloe shook her curls again and turned a piercing glance in my direction. I studied the jars of sweets on the shelf and pretended not to be listening.

'When's the funeral d'you know?' Mrs Parsloe enquired in lowered tones. Then raising her voice, 'A half of cheddar please, Dot.'

'The 'Mejum' do you dear, or the Strong?'

'Oh, Medium, Dot, please. Rod likes the Strong, but the girls won't eat it.'

I sympathised with the Parsloe girls; the Strong cheese could be smelled from fifty yards away!

'Next Thursd'y I b'lieve.' Dot deftly cut the wedge of cheese and plonked it on the scales.

'Nine ounces, Marjorie, is that orlright?'

'Yes, that'll do, Dot.'

'A packet of Daz and half of margarine,' murmured Mrs Parsloe scanning her long list.

'They were sayin' in the post office,' said Dot as she

reached for the box of Daz on the shelf behind her, 'that Mrs C. had gone up to bed an' when 'er 'usband din't come up, she went down to look fer 'im and found 'im **dead**.'

'She found 'im **dead**! Oooh I *say!*'

'Stone cold 'e wuz an' all.' Dot's voice assumed hushed tones as she imparted this important titbit.

'Ooh, I *say!*' tutted Mrs Parsloe in shocked disbelief. Looking round at the shop stock to see if the information had been taken in.

The door handle rattled and the bell jangled loudly as someone entered the shop.

'Ere, I come in 'ere an hour ago an' you wuz in 'ere then; 're you gonna be in 'ere all day?'

'Just six rashers of the streaky, Dot, and I think that'll be all for now.' Mrs Parsloe hastily paid her bill and giving a resentful glance to the waiting customers as she gathered up her shopping, trotted self-importantly out.

Almost everybody used the shop at some time or another, even Mr Z. who worked on a farm and always trailed manure on his boots wherever he walked. There was such a pervasive smell of it that Dot would make him stay outside and call out his order from the open doorway.

Sometimes our elderly neighbour, John Reeve, would send us to the shop for his Woodbine cigarettes. 'Don't tell sister,' he'd say, referring to his bossy sister at Yew Tree Farm who did not approve of his smoking habit.

On one occasion my brother M had been sent to the shop to buy cigarettes for John Reeve, and when he didn't return after fifteen minutes, B and I went to look for him. We found M searching the grass verge. 'Lost anything, M?' enquired B.

'No,' replied M, continuing to scan the verge.

'Hey,' I exclaimed, 'look what I've found!' I snatched up the ten shilling note from amongst the grass.

'Well done, Ceri', teased B, 'let's go and spend some of it!'

We laughed as we both knew it was the note M had lost and we would not dream of spending it.

'Hey, no, you can't do that, I lost it,' admitted M. So we gave it back, but when John Reeve heard about it he gave me sixpence.

Despite the long wait to be served, the shop was an important part of village life and sold a good variety of basic foodstuff and household items, as well as the usual jars of sweets and penny chews. One could buy four fruit salad or liquorice chews for a penny then. Liquorice bootlaces were also good value as they were about three feet six inches long (just under a metre) and could be used as a skipping rope first and then eaten afterwards. On one occasion when I was about seven, my brother M bought me a liquorice bootlace for my birthday. He hid it away in his bedroom the day before and could not resist taking it out of its hiding place at regular intervals to gloat over it. However, each time he did this he took a few bites of the bootlace. When he finally gave the bootlace to me the following day it was only about five inches long!

Our parents generally disapproved of any sweets

which turned our tongues a violent shade of blue or green, or gob stoppers which had to be removed from the mouth every ten seconds so that the new colour could be admired. I usually spent ages deciding between pear drops and aniseed balls, mint humbugs or mint imperials. I don't think choosing bags of sweets in a supermarket gives the same pleasure as standing before a row of jars full of brightly coloured sweets. In this instance things really were better in the old days.

CHAPTER 16

THE WOMEN'S INSTITUTE

Little Somerford had a flourishing Women's Institute and almost all the village ladies attended the monthly meeting. It was always an interesting meeting; there were talks and competitions and a small raffle and it was a good chance to speak to neighbours and hear the latest gossip. The members took it in turns to provide refreshments with a rota of three or four members providing cakes.

Our mother went out to work and was always busy gardening, so that she often forget about her turn to provide a cake until the day itself. I remember one amusing occasion when my mother made a last minute sponge cake, and although she was a very good cook, it came out flat. There was no time to make another. In despair she sent me into the garden to pick a few strawberries. Sliced strawberries were sandwiched in the middle of the cake with icing sugar and a few placed on top of the cake for decoration, held on by a little icing.

'I'll probably be bringing it home,' sighed my mother sadly, 'nobody will want to eat this!'

We weren't quite as upset at this prospect as our

mother, and watched hungrily as the cake was carefully wrapped for transportation to the village hall.

Later that evening, when the ladies of the Women's Institute queued up for their tea and cake, my mother saw with horror that Mrs Lutley, the rector's wife, had chosen a piece of her sponge. She braced herself for some disappointed comment, the sponge was clearly flat!

'Who made this delicious strawberry shortcake?' demanded Mrs Lutley in a loud voice, forking another morsel into her mouth. Hastily smothering her laughter, my mother was able to pretend her cake was meant to be a strawberry shortcake all along. After the favourable comment everyone wanted a piece and withing a few minutes it had been eaten. My mother did not even get to the front of the queue in time to get a piece for herself.

Whenever it was my mother's turn to provide refreshments we always suggested that she make another strawberry shortcake!

CHAPTER 17

BRINKWORTH BROOK

Brinkworth Brook, a small tributary of the Avon, ran south-east of the village, about half a mile from our house and we spent many happy afternoons down there.

First we had to have bait. To begin with this was just pellets of damp bread, but M, a keen fisherman, wanted to catch more than minnows and as usual he required my help.

'Come on, Ceri,' he'd say one evening. 'Put that book away, we need some worms.'

'Well, you get them. I'm reading.'

'No! I need you to get the worms while I hold the torch! There'll be hundreds out now, come on!' Clutching an empty baked bean tin in one hand and a torch in the other, he led the way through the kitchen on to the old scullery and out to the front garden. There we slowly traversed the lawn, M shining the torch on the wet grass and me picking up the worms which crawled around the tin seeking a way out. Earth and a few rotting leaves were added so that they had some food and shelter and then the tin was put into the old wash house until the next day.

My brothers had home-made fishing rods, made by our father, which consisted of tall bamboo canes with rings made from safety pins bound on with strong thread which was then varnished to make it waterproof. To this was added a reel, line, float, lead weights and a hook. I only had a jam jar on a string which was only suitable for catching minnows, sticklebacks and the occasional bullhead.

None of us could swim so we were never allowed down the river alone, and we had to promise to keep within the three bridges which was an area covered by two fields. The water here was never deeper than our waists and in many places was less than a foot deep. Nevertheless, the water teemed with life.

Silver dace gleamed in the water as they swam to and fro. Hordes of minnows flickered in the sunlight, and if you paddled in the shallows, stone loach, camouflaged against the pebbles, nibbled at your toes, while the bulbous, fierce-looking bullheads lurked in the shadows, raising their spiny gills at any perceived threat. We fished mostly in the shallow area near the humped road bridge where there was a small gravelly beach where cattle came down to drink. Here the stream ran swiftly, bubbling and gurgling over the pebbles until it flowed under the bridge, over the smooth green-weeded shelf of the weir into the depths of the larger pool under the ancient willows which overhung the bank. From there it flowed on through the lush water meadows beyond.

Green and blue dragon flies darted above the water or

settled briefly on the rosebay willow herb at the edge of the brook. Water mint, crowfoot and teasels jostled for space at the water's edge, water voles swam upstream to their holes in the bank, and mud, water mint and river weed scented the air.

Behind us the meadow grass was carpeted with buttercups, purple vetch and ox-eye daisies. It was a magical place.

Sometimes we made a small pond area at the side of the stream where our catch could be kept for half an hour before being allowed to swim off. If we tired of fishing we could wade up the stream, but usually I preferred to sit amongst the water mint, idly watching the dragonflies settle for a fleeting moment on one of the water plants before darting away in their seemingly endless dance. I'd watch the silver dace glinting in the green depths or the water boatmen skating across the surface of the brook, while M cast his line hoping to catch a chub or perch in the deeper water. Here clouds of midges danced in the air and the swallows swooped low to catch them, a sure sign of rain. Then came the exciting moment when the float dipped under the water's surface and then bobbed up again, indicating a bite. Usually it was a dace or a gudgeon which was thrown back.

On rare occasions I was allowed to borrow a rod, but I hated baiting the hook with live worms, while M was wary of the fierce looking bullheads which he caught, and made me take them off the hook and slip them back into the water. They are strange looking fish, blotchy and mottled in colour to blend in with the pebbles and river mud, and their spiny gills make them look particularly fearsome, yet I admired them for their bravery when caught; they are bold little fish.

Sometimes passing villagers would lean over the bridge to chat to us. On one occasion when I was fishing with M and his friend Nigel, a stranger stopped and asked questions which made us feel uneasy, and M put down his rod and came over to whisper, 'Put that jam jar down, just leave it. Listen, when I say *run*, run, ok?'

I nodded and a few seconds later the order came. We raced back across the tussocky grass. I was last as usual and begged the boys to wait for me. They slowed slightly, yelling at me to hurry up, and casting anxious glances behind at the stranger who seemed to want to go after us. We all made it to the field gate which led to another small field near to our home. We were not allowed down the brook for a few weeks and our mother walked down with us to rescue M's rod and the jam jar which we had had to leave behind.

Sometimes we walked a little further upstream where the brook meandered creating several deeper pools, but the water was still well within our depth. Here chub and perch could sometimes be caught. There was one bridge a field away from the road with an iron railing. It was perfect for games like *Poohsticks.* On the second field was a World War II pill box which we sometimes played in or climbed on its grassy roof. Further up was the third bridge and just in front of this the stream widened into a large pool about three feet deep. It was fed by a small noisy waterfall pouring over a rocky shelf. Beyond this the stream was much wider forming deep pools where water lilies grew. We were never allowed there on our own and were careful to keep within our imposed boundary of the third bridge by the rocky waterfall.

When I was about eleven the stream was dredged, much to our horror as the beautiful meanders were evened out, but the earth dredged up from the bed of the stream contained many fossils, belemnites and ammonites which provided a new source of interest for us and we had several expeditions to look for them.

CHAPTER 18

SOMERFORD FRIENDS

Wendy Barnes

Known affectionately by her mum as 'Ole Litt'lun', Wendy Barnes was a year younger than me. A slim girl with beautiful chestnut hair and a creamy gold complexion, she lived with her parents and older sister, Julie, at a house at the top of Somerford Hill. There was a big age gap between the two girls so I was often asked to their house because – as her mother, Stella, put it – I kept Wendy out of mischief. Stella was very kind to me and always included me in family meals and sweet rations.

They had a swing in their garden and since Wendy and I both wanted to sit on it we balanced a short plank across the seat and sat one at each end of that. We used to swing and talk for hours. On one occasion when I was eight, we decided to go for a walk, and as it looked like rain I took my coat, but Wendy did not want to wear hers so she took an umbrella. When the rain started we were several fields away from her house so we shared the coat, each putting an arm into it and holding the umbrella above us. This was fine until we came to a barbed wire fence. The contortions we went through in order to get between the strands of barbed wire without removing our coat were hilarious.

Wendy usually had an acquisition in mind, whether it was a telescope or a new tennis racquet which she wanted her parents to get for her. On wet days our games of Monopoly and Buccaneer or cards were fiercely competitive as neither of us liked to lose. Once or twice in very hot weather we camped out in their back garden. On these occasions we copied many of the school stories we read by having a midnight feast of cake and greengages.

Once Wendy had a small bird whistle, one that trilled just like a small bird. We took this with us when we went to post a letter for her mother. Having posted the letter in the box at Somerford Corner in the centre of the village, we walked back to The Hill. At that moment we spied Mr R, a sweet, gentlemanly man with a quiet manner, going for his afternoon walk. Concealing the whistle in her hand, Wendy blew it, just as Mr R was approaching a tree. He stopped and stared around looking for the bird which had trilled. Wendy blew the whistle again and Mr R stared intently at the tree canopy, trying to see the bird. We burst into giggles which I hastily pretended was something to do with a trailing shoelace.

'Hurry up, Vyner,' teased Wendy.

'Hang on a minute, my lace is undone,' I replied loudly enough for Mr R to hear.

Re-tying my laces gave us an excuse to linger, and as

Fern Cottage front garden

Fern Cottage back of house

Fern Cottage showing part of kitchen garden

Yew Tree Farm (reproduced with permission of Mr Oliver Jones Davies)

Street Farm from the road

Sunnyside, opposite Fern Cottage (reproduced with permission of Julie Frayling)

The Reeve family in 1914. It was taken because William and John had volunteered and the family wanted a record before they went to war. Unfortunately, Jane's daughter Ellen (Nellie) was not included in family photos as her grandfather would not allow it.

The photo shows the family gathered in the small paddock next to the front garden of Street Farm Little Somerford. The gable of the big stone barn can be seen in the background. This paddock now has several houses built over it, but the barn roof can still just be seen from the road.

Back row (left to right): James, William, John and Lizzy
Middle row: Jane, Mr Reeve, Mrs Reeve, Charles and Kate
Front: Ernest

John Reeve in soldier's uniform, WWI

The Reeve family c.1890–91 in the front doorway of Street Farm. The small boy standing between his father's knees is John Reeve. The two youngest Reeves who survived infancy, Kate and Ernest, had not yet been born.
Left to right: James, Mr Reeve holding John, Jane (standing), Mrs Reeve holding Lizzy, William and Charles

A tracker clears snow on The Hill in Little Somerford, in 1963 (reproduced with permission of Martyn Scott)

Looking up Little Somerford hill, January 1963
(reproduced with permission of Martyn Scott)

Looking down The Hill, January 1963
(reproduced with permission of Martyn Scott)

Little Somerford Corner in 2022

Little Somerford school in 2022

Wendy blew the whistle again I surreptitiously glanced across the road at Mr R who was carefully peering this way and that into the tree. Shaking with laughter, Wendy passed the whistle to me. I blew it gently twice and Mr R looked across, but we seemed to be having a private conversation entirely unconnected to the bird song he was hearing. By this time we were both crying with silent laughter, but we also knew that we had to move in order to avoid suspicion, so we walked on a few yards before giving a final trill on the whistle. After a minute we glanced over our shoulders, Mr R was still staring at the tree hoping to see the mystery bird. We tried the whistle again, halfway up The Hill when we caught up with a lady going to visit a friend, but this lady was not deceived and just gave us a suspicious look, even though she could not see the whistle. Nevertheless, we laughed all the way home.

Christine Cuss

On Saturdays, from the age of six, I walked up to Cleverton where Mrs Cuss and my friend Christine would be waiting to see me safely across the busy Swindon road. Cleverton is a tiny hamlet about a mile away from Little Somerford. Christine attended our village school and was the same age as I was. There was nobody in Cleverton her age, so her mother arranged for me to spend the day with Christine.

Christine's parents were keen gardeners and had a large garden which was beautifully maintained. There was an extensive vegetable patch which was tended by Mr Cuss, and Mrs Cuss was in charge of the attractive borders of dahlias and chrysanthemums.

There was a small paddock with a pond where one summer, Chris and I spent several days watching a blackcap which had nested nearby and spent much of its time singing on a hawthorn branch which overhung the pond. There was a great deal of bird and insect life there and one favourite summer occupation was watching and counting the many butterflies on the buddleia bush.

Christine had a dog, a black curly coated retriever called Blackie, who lived outside in a kennel. We often played with him. Chris liked to wind up the old fashioned gramophone and play a record to which she would dance around with her dog. Sometimes we went for a walk to admire the foal in the field down the road, or made a house out of the cane wigwam her father had built for his runner beans. Mrs Cuss was a wonderful cook and there was always a delicious lunch and later Mrs Cuss's sponge cake, and homemade jam for tea. After that they would accompany me to the main road and I'd hurry down Clay Street and up the road to our house.

Once I asked Christine what someone had said about something and she replied 'He didn't say cat, dog nor pig'

When I asked her why she had said that, she replied that her mother and her cousins used that expression. On investigation it turned out to be a saying originating in the Collingbourne family who were known to Christine's mother.

The Collingbournes were descendants of one William Collingbourne who was hung, drawn and quartered in 1484 for allegedly putting up a lampoon on the door of St Paul's Cathedral. It said:

The Cat, the Rat and Lovell our Dog Doe Ruleth all England under a Hog

The Cat was a reference to William Catesby, the Rat was Richard Ratcliffe and Lovell was Lord Lovell, whose heraldic crest was a wolf. These men were counsellors to Richard III. The Hog referred to Richard III whose emblem was a white boar.

The saying: *'He didn't say cat, dog nor pig,'* either refers to the fact that the Collingbourne family believed their kinsman to be innocent, or that he did not say anything to defend himself at his trial.

It is very interesting that this saying is still used today by some people in north Wiltshire where the Collingbourne family still live.

Susan

When I was about nine years old, I sometimes played with a girl called Susan, whose mother was housekeeper to Mrs Chamberlain who lived at Hill House, a very large mansion on the edge of the village. Once when I went to call for Susan, who lived in a flat in the house, Mrs Chamberlain answered the door and called up to Susan that she had a visitor. However, Mrs Chamberlain remained at the door to talk to me while I waited. She showed me a large black umbrella which was in a stand by the front door.

'It's a family heirloom,' she told me, 'we're very proud of it. My father-in-law was Prime Minister and used this umbrella when he went to meet Hitler in Munich. You won't understand now, but you will when you are older,' she said. 'Here, hold it.' She opened the umbrella and passed it to me to hold. 'When you are grown up, you will be able to say you held the Munich umbrella!'

I held the umbrella and duly waved it around for a few minutes, unaware at the time of what an honour it was. My parents were very interested to hear about it and told me how lucky I was to hold a piece of history.

Christine and I went on to Malmesbury Grammar school together and I am still in touch with both Wendy and Christine, over sixty years later.

CHAPTER 19

A FEW SOMERFORD CHARACTERS

Cecil & Kathleen Gawthropp

Cecil Gawthropp was a tall red cheeked country farmer with a bluff and hearty manner. I first encountered him one day after school when I was about seven years old. I had just been escorted across Somerford corner by our teacher, Mrs Perks, and started walking home up the footpath, when the throaty roar of a vehicle disturbed the peace and I looked up to see a blue Ford tractor pulling a very smelly dung-spreader. Lumps of dung were flung in all directions and a breathless little black Jack Russell dog, called Joker, came running along the road, his tongue lolling and sides heaving in his efforts to catch up with his master. The engine grumbled to a standstill as the tractor driver pulled up with a jerk on the opposite side of the road. The smell of petrol combined with a strong odour of cow dung hung in the air and small pieces of dung continued to fall for several minutes.

The driver turned to me and bellowed in a voice audible to anyone within two hundred yards: 'Hello, Missy, had the cane today? Ha Haa Haa,' he roared, slapping his knee at his own joke. 'Yer father'll lather ye.'

I was a shy child and blushed scarlet. Everyone in the vicinity could hear him and I was mortally embarrassed. The least suspicion of any misbehaviour on my part would invoke parental wrath. I hurried on, blushing again as I passed smiling neighbours who had clearly overheard Cecil's remarks.

Despite his teasing manner Cecil Gawthropp was a very kind man and well liked by his neighbours.

A few months later I met Mrs Gawthropp, a tall, smartly dressed, woman with short auburn hair.

Mrs Gawthropp was passing our garden laden down with shopping bags, having got off the village bus at the end of the street. My mother was in the garden and saw her staggering along under this enormous weight of shopping.

'Ceri, come and help,' called my mother, insisting I help carry the bags despite Mrs Gawthropp saying she could manage. 'She's used to helping,' my mother replied reassuringly.

As Mrs Gawthropp obviously couldn't manage she accepted my help. East End Farm was a steep twenty minute walk so I took one handle of Mrs Gawthropp's heavy shopping bag while she held the other and two other bags and between us we lugged it up the lane. Mrs Gawthropp was very grateful and gave me a bar of chocolate which pleased me very much. This incident obviously impressed her and after that she always chatted to me, much to the surprise of some of our neighbours who had not really got to know her well.

The following winter there was heavy snow forecast. My mother and I were walking back from the bus stop when we met Cecil Gawthropp, 'Cold weather, Mrs Vyner, it'll snow tonight. Eight or nine inches they say! Your children going sledging?'

'I'm afraid we don't have a sledge any more. My husband used it for something else.'

'Oh, they must go sledging! They can use our old sledge. It's hanging in the barn; Robert doesn't use it any more. We'll want it back, mind, but they won't do any harm if they have it for a few days. Send them up tomorrow,' he instructed, 'About ten thirty'll do. I'll have it ready.' With a wave of his large hand he carried on up the lane.

It snowed hard overnight and there was eight to ten inches of snow on the road when, next morning, wrapped up in our warmest clothes and muffled in hats and scarves, we waded through the snow up East End Lane. We were very familiar with neighbouring farms but we had never been in Mr Gawthropp's farmyard. Their solid, handsome red-bricked farmhouse was nearly at the end of East End Lane. Mr Gawthropp was expecting us and came out of the barn as we arrived. Joker, the Jack Russell, barked excitedly at our arrival and scampered towards us uttering doggy threats, but a word from his master calmed him and he wagged his tail instead. 'It's all ready for you,' said Mr Gawthropp. 'I've waxed the runners and put some new rope on it.' He had obviously gone to a lot of trouble and we were delighted, thanking him profusely.

'Make sure, you let the Little Maid ride home on it,' he said sternly, eyeing my brothers, 'Don't you let her walk all the way home in this snow!' he insisted. 'Here,' he called to me, 'you sit on there now, Missy, an' they can tow you home.'

With more polite thanks and promises to return the sledge in a few days, I was towed out of the yard. East End Farm was at the top of a steep sloping lane which wound down round several sharp bends to the village almost half a mile below. My brothers pulled the sledge to the corner of the bend, then M climbed on behind me, clutching me under the arms and holding the steering rope. B hauled himself aboard behind M and pushed us off with his feet.

The weight of the three of us gave the sledge momentum. The beautifully waxed runners carved their way through the untouched snow in the middle of the road and very soon we picked up speed.

The sledge soared and dipped, carrying us down the slope, round the first bend and along the straight. Flying along now, we picked up speed, sailing round the next bend, down a dip in the lane and along the second slope. The cold wind rushed by, reddening our cheeks. We gasped in amazement as the sledge continued rushing round the last long bend and down the last few yards until it came to a slow halt in a small snowdrift at the side of the lane. We had had the sledge ride of our lives.

Mrs Dredge

Mrs Dredge lived about a mile away from our house, at Idover on the Dauntsey Road. She was a large lady with grey, bobbed curly hair and a long face with rosy cheeks. She knew all the village news and often stopped to talk to my mother.

Mrs Dredge seemed to be worried that I would get lost if I wandered too far from home. To be fair to her, the walk down to Idover was a lonely bit of road and a dark wood had to be passed which I did not much care for. Whenever I went to play with our friends the Taylors who lived at that time a few houses past Mrs Dredge's house I would encounter her.

'What're you doin' down 'ere?' she would demand, rushing down her path to the gate and running into the road to stop me.

'I'm going to see the Taylors,' I'd reply politely, even though it was none of her business. The four Taylor children – Kathleen, Barry, Christopher and Douglas – were at school with us at that time.

'Go home, you'll get lost down 'ere,' she'd say.

'No, I'm going to play at the Taylors' house!'

'You'll get lost! I bet your mother doesn't know you're all the way down 'ere,' insisted Mrs Dredge.

'Yes, she does, and I know where I'm going,' I replied trying to dodge round her.

Eventually she let me go on my way after threatening to report me to my mother. However, since I had my mother's permission to visit the Taylors I wasn't worried about Mrs Dredge, and I complained to my mother about *her!*

On one occasion I was going to a birthday party at the Taylor's house and Mrs Dredge, having interrogated me, did not believe me, and insisted on accompanying me there to see if I really was going. Mrs Taylor was not very pleased, so after that she did not try to stop me, but always warned me not to get lost. Looking back now, I realise how lucky we were that villagers kept an eye out for us and had our wellbeing at heart.

Mrs Stoneham

Mrs Stoneham, a tall, good looking woman with bright red curls, was another neighbour who lived in one of the railway cottages on the Dauntsey Road. She was brought up in the village and her parents lived on The Hill. She was always out and about in the village and when I was a very small child I would stand at our gate and watch the neighbours through the railings.

I would observe Mrs Stoneham pushing her son in his pushchair as she walked to the shop and then back again, then walking past on her way up to her parents' house and back, or walking briskly up the road to some village event or to see a friend. To me, as a four year old, she seemed to walk backwards and forwards all day, much like the shunting trains I could see in the station yard, which moved trucks backwards and forwards in much the same energetic manner. I did not know her name at that time, so I called her *Mrs Shunting Train* and I would call to my mother or my brothers, 'Come and see, come and see Mrs Shunting Train', and I would rush to the gate to watch her go by again.

Mr and Mrs Scott

Fred and Eva Scott, like so many people in the village, were locals and extremely hardworking people. Mr Scott did farm work while Mrs Scott was the school caretaker. When they retired they lived next door to us in a new house built on part of the little orchard next to our garden.

Mr Scott was a very keen gardener. One day, not having seen them in recent weeks my mother stopped to chat to Mr Scott, thinking she might hear some fascinating snippet of village gossip.

'Hello, Mr Scott,' she began.

''Ow're yer potatoes doin' Mrs Vyner?' came the reply.

'Did Mr Scott have any news?' I enquired later.

'No, he didn't tell me anything', complained my mother. 'He was only interested in my potatoes!'

We quite often passed a bowl of gooseberries or a bag of apples over the hedge to them and invariably a few cabbage seedlings or young winter greens plants wrapped in damp newspaper would be found on our doorstep.

Mrs Scott was always very busy. 'How are you, Mrs Scott?' asked my mother one day.

'Oooh, Oi bin scortin' around all day, you!' came the exhausted reply. This expression passed into family history and I still use it when talking to them.

Scortin = scorching or rushing around

Ron and Millie Thomas

When I was thirteen I was walking down The Street to a bazaar in the village hall. I heard someone calling my name so I stopped and turned round. It was Mrs Thomas, a sweet and lovely lady who lived on The Hill. She asked if she could walk down with me, which surprised me as I knew that she had lived in the village all her life and knew everybody.

As we passed the church and the old railway bridge came in sight, she exclaimed, 'I hate walking down here, the sight of that railway bridge upsets me so much. My brother was killed just along there on the railway line.'

She pointed to a place a few yards from the bridge.

'Oh, how terrible! It must have been awful for you,' I sympathised.

'It was. He worked on the railway, see, and there was a blizzard, and the men were clearing the line so the train could get through. The snow muffled the noise of the engine and it was snowing so hard that they didn't see it coming and the driver couldn't see them, and he was killed. Richard Harford he was called. You can see the plaque they put up.'

She indicated a metal plaque at the side of the bridge which recorded the tragedy. We stopped to read it.

Millie Thomas sighed and said, 'I cried for two weeks, it was Ron who made me stop. We were walking out then, and he came to see me. He came several times, but I wouldn't see him, I was too upset. But after two weeks he came round and said, *"Millie, it's a terrible thing that's happened, but crying won't bring him back, so you've got to stop now,"* so I did, but I still hate walking down here on my own. Thank you for your company.'

I smiled sympathetically. In thoughtful silence we walked into the bazaar. I felt honoured that Mrs Thomas had wanted to share her story with me.

Ron Thomas, Millie's husband was a kind and friendly man who was once signalman and porter at Little Somerford station. When the station closed, Mr Thomas retired and his tiny garden halfway up The Hill was filled with station memorabilia which would be the envy of many a collector today. Signals, set to indicate that a train was approaching, railway lamps, an enamel village sign and an old railway bench took pride of place on his tiny lawn. Flowers were an afterthought.

Ron Thomas had in the 1960s a black collie cross dog called George which accompanied him to the pub and enjoyed a drink of beer as much as the regulars.

Once when I was a student, I was walking up The Hill when I met Mr Thomas whom I had not seen for a few months. I noticed that he had grown a beard since I had seen him last. I stopped to say hello. After greeting me he asked, 'Whaddya think of my beard then?' brushing his fingers through the bushy growth on his chin.

'It's not as good as my dad's,' I smiled.

'Ah, but he's been cultivating that for years!' he replied in a disappointed tone.

Mrs Isles, Frank Knight and George Isles

Mrs Isles was a lovely lady, plump, good hearted and

kind. Having lived in the village all her life she was a fount of village knowledge. She was always very friendly and chatty and used to tell me about her childhood in a small house next to Kingsmead mill. Now she lived in a snug, stone built cottage at the bottom of East End Lane. Her house was beautifully kept.

Mrs Isles had a birthday in the second week of January and my mother always asked me to pick a bunch of snowdrops from our garden for her as they were always out by then. I would pick a few ivy leaves to set them off and then take them over. Snowdrops are unlucky to have indoors and country people are rather superstitious about these things so I think she kept them on her outside windowsill so that she could still enjoy them without risking the supposed bad luck. The bowl of strawberries I took over in June was even more appreciated. We also helped Mrs Isles if it was her turn to do the church flowers. Her garden was much smaller and neater and there was always something out in our garden and plenty of greenery too.

In the cottage next door lived two of her brothers, Frank Knight and George Isles. Frank was her brother and George was her brother-in-law. These two men were elderly when we knew them and did not get on with each other. They quarrelled a lot so that Mrs Isles often had to go into their cottage to 'sort them out' as she described it.

Frank Knight, the eldest, was a small, slightly built man who always dressed smartly in a grey suit and trilby hat and walked with a stick. He was very deaf and sadly it was almost impossible to have any conversation with him because most people could not understand what he was trying to say. His conversations involved much muttering into his moustache and waving his walking stick in the air.

George was a cheerful character who enjoyed a drink and wandered back from the pub in a merry mood, often muttering to himself. He was a friendly person and always said hello if we passed him in the street.

Old George, as he was affectionately known, had been a porter at Little Somerford station. One aspect of his job he had evidently enjoyed was chatting to passengers. One day he stopped to chat to a lady who was waiting for the Swindon train. She was going to visit her sister and on hearing this George reassured her: 'Don't you worry, my dear, I'll make sure you get the right train.' When the next train came into the station George seized her bag and hurried to open the door. Quickly handing the lady and her bag into the carriage he closed the door and waved her off, only to realise a few minutes later that that was the London train which went straight through to Paddington and did not stop at Swindon where the lady was heading. Poor old George was never allowed to forget the incident which caused much amusement in the village. It is still talked of today!

On one occasion, when I was thirteen, Old George had broken some bones in his hand. Naturally it was very painful and George flatly refused to go to his hospital appointment fearing further pain. Mrs Isles was at her wits' end, so she came to our house to ask if I could have a word with George, as I'd broken my elbow two weeks previously and had my arm in plaster from palm to shoulder.

A few minutes later she returned with George. 'Look, George,' scolded Mrs Isles, 'Ceri's got her arm in plaster, and she's not afraid to go to the hospital on her own, so you can jolly well go!'

I had to reassure George that I would be going to the hospital that Thursday too. Two days later, George reluctantly climbed into the ambulance which went around all the villages and took patients to their appointments at the Royal United Hospital in Bath. Throughout the journey, poor old George repeatedly asked me if the removal of his plaster was going to hurt and I tried to reassure him as much as I could, though inwardly shuddering at the sight of his badly swollen and twisted fingers. I knew his appointment would be a painful experience, but I could only tell him otherwise.

CHAPTER 20

INTRODUCTION TO THE REEVES

I have included as much detail as possible about the Reeves because for nearly a hundred years they were an important farming family in Little Somerford. They lived through times of great social upheaval and change and their story is so interesting that I think It is important that it is written down.

The Reeve family moved to Street Farm, Little Somerford in 1888. They farmed there until 1921 when they bought Yew Tree Farm just up the road and moved there. I was told that this was because the land was better at Yew Tree Farm.

After the First World War, William and John, the second and fourth sons, and their sister Eliza went to farm at Union Farm, Dauntsey, two miles away. They rented this in 1920 from Wiltshire County Council who made farms available for veterans to rent after the First World War. In 1958, William, John and Eliza retired and moved back to Little Somerford to Sunnyside, a

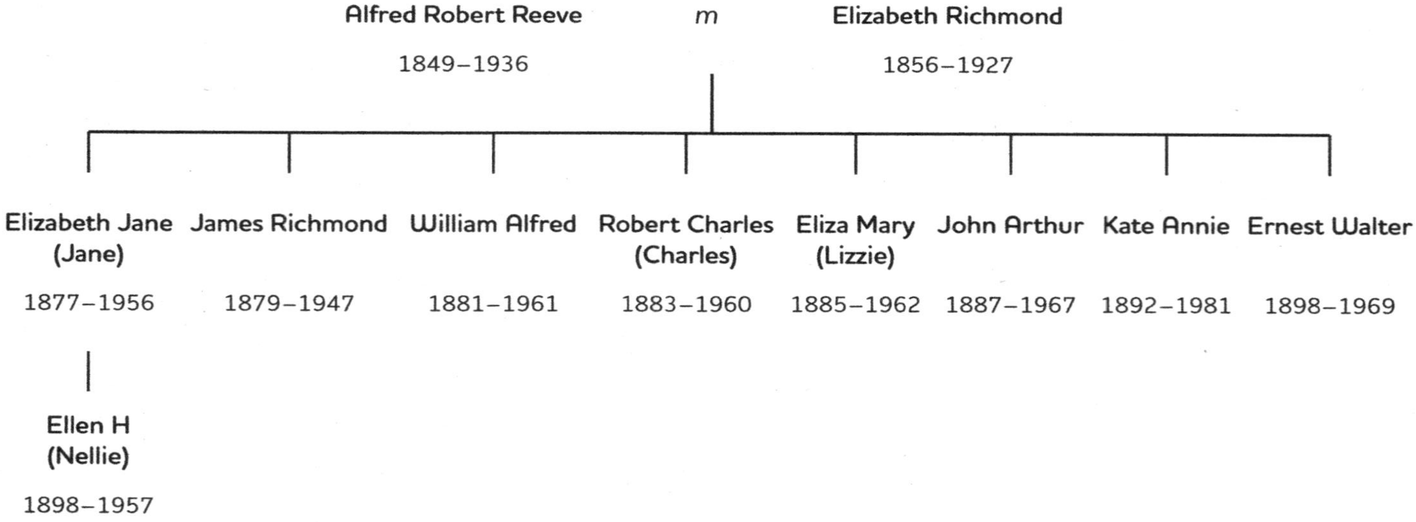

The Reeve family

cottage next to Yew Tree Farm which was also owned by the Reeves.

The Reeves remained largely Victorians. They farmed with carthorses until 1958 and although after that there was a tractor at Yew Tree Farm, none of the Reeves ever learned to drive it. Nellie Reeve's Vauxhall car stayed in the garage after her death in the 1950s and was only occasionally driven by a friend of the family, who would sometimes take Kate Reeve for a drive on Sunday afternoons. I was usually asked to accompany her.

I think it is very sad that none of the Reeves ever married and the family died out. Kate Reeve, the last surviving member of the family died in 1981.

Alfred Robert Reeve and Elizabeth Reeve

'Father's word was law!' is how Kate Reeve remembered her father. Mrs Iles, an elderly neighbour who had lived in the village all her life, told me that Mr Reeve had ruled his family with a 'rod of iron'.

We never knew Mr Reeve senior, but his influence on his children extended long after his death and well into their old age.

Alfred Reeve had farmed at Church Farm, Brinkworth, where he was churchwarden, but moved his growing family to Street Farm, Little Somerford in 1888. Lizzie Reeve, his second daughter, said that she remembered sitting on the laden cart when she was about three years old, as they drove down Clay Street to their new home. She was wrapped in a red blanket and sat beside her mother who had her then youngest child, John, in her arms as he was only a tiny baby.

The older Reeve boys, James and William helped to drive the cattle down from Brinkworth to Little Somerford.

Anecdotal evidence suggests that Mr Reeve was a proud man with ambitions for his family. His eldest daughter, Jane, was educated at a private school for young ladies at Great Somerford; and the others went on from the village school to the Grammar school in Malmesbury which was then fee paying. The fee being one shilling and six pence per week. Kate, the third daughter was allowed to have a career.

Kate always said: 'Father loved children,' which was just as well as he and Elizabeth had eleven, three of whom died in infancy, as many did in those days.

The children were strictly brought up, everyone having to do their bit on the farm or in the house from the age of four. In the family photos you see Mr Reeve, a tall man with an oblong face and sad, heavy-lidded eyes, and droopy moustache. He is surrounded by his family, and in the background the weeping pear which he planted on the front lawn of his new farm. A tree which was perhaps symbolic of the family's later decline as none of the children ever had the chance to marry and only Kate, and later Will, John and Lizzie, ever really escaped their father's total domination.

Alfred was inevitably very upset when Jane had an illicit affair with an animal food delivery man and became pregnant. All the Reeve children were instructed to refer to Jane's daughter as *'My sister, Nellie'* if they mentioned her, and they still spoke of her in this way in the 1960s and indeed corrected themselves if they started saying 'Nellie …' they hastily amended it to 'My sister, Nellie …'

However, Mr Reeve did say, many years later, when the division of the farm was being discussed, that Nellie should inherit her mother Jane's share in the farm. Villagers told us that after Nellie's arrival, the Reeve children, even those who were grown up, were hardly ever allowed out. They went to a village event once a year and that was that, except for church on Sundays.

All the Reeve children were expected to work on the farm all day, every day. They were never paid wages. In 1921, Alfred and Elizabeth Reeve moved from Street Farm to Yew Tree Farm – just up the road – with Jane, James, Charles, Ernest and Nellie. Kate lived there during the school holidays when she was home from teaching.

Alfred's wife, Elizabeth liked nice things. She inherited good furniture and clocks from her relations, which would suggest that her family, the Richmonds, were comfortably off. They had cousins who had a piano shop in Cirencester. Elizabeth had a brother, Thomas Richmond, of whom she was very fond. He went out to Australia in the 1820s to earn his fortune, after being jilted by a local girl. He wrote to Elizabeth for a short time, but then his letters stopped abruptly. They later heard that he had met with an accident and been killed by a piece of wood from a wood sawing machine.

In late middle age, Elizabeth was stout in appearance

with an oval face and dark hair parted in the middle and tied back in a bun. Matronly is the word which best describes her, but any woman who has had eleven children is entitled to lose her figure! She was very good at needlework and I have a black silk scarf which she made in 1901 to attend the memorial service held in the village church after the death of Queen Victoria.

Mrs Reeve managed the dairy and kept hens. Eggs were sold to the village shop. She used to sell the milk to London and sometimes they got a telegram: '*Keep the milk three days*' so they then had to make butter and cheese. Mrs Reeve had to put rennet in the milk to turn it and the whey was given to the pigs. The butter was sold and the milk made into cheese. Wiltshire Loaf, a delicious crumbly, creamy cheese was the one she made.

Jane Reeve

Elizabeth Jane Reeve, known as Jane, was the eldest daughter of the Reeve family. When she was four months old her mother took her to visit her maternal grandfather, James Richmond. He died as he was holding his tiny granddaughter in his arms as he sat by the fire and her mother just managed to catch her as she was dropped.

Jane was educated at Brinkworth Primary School and a private school at Pond Farm, Great Somerford from the age of twelve to fourteen. This was a kind of finishing school, which was then owned by some people called Teagle. Jane's parents wanted her to be a well brought up young lady and superior to most of the other girls in the village.

As a young woman, Jane Reeve was very good looking. Jane had an affair in her twenties and this resulted in her daughter, Ellen, known as Nellie. Jane was apparently very protective of Nellie and did not allow her brothers and sisters to make fun of her in any way.

As she grew older, Jane did a lot of the household work. She looked after her younger brothers and sisters, especially Kate, as well as Nellie.

Farmers had to provide beer for all the hired men in those days and Jane did all the brewing. She had to be up at four-thirty in the morning to light the fires under the coppers to heat the water for the brewing. A copper was a very large bowl-shaped pan, often made of copper, set in a brick surround. It was backed by a chimney and had a grate underneath it so that a fire could be lit and water heated in the copper for washing or other household purposes.

The brew was poured into big pans and taken out onto the lawn to cool. Brewing was frequent, especially before the harvest when extra men would be hired to help.

Jane inherited her mother's talent for housekeeping. Her jam was being enjoyed by her surviving brothers and sisters for years after her death. She also used to make wonderful soft toy animals for Nellie, one of which, a toy dog, was brought down from their attic and given to me many years later. I can remember Jane as a very old lady.

James Reeve

James Richmond Reeve was the eldest son, named after his maternal grandfather, James Richmond. The other children used to tease him about his fancy middle name. In photos he looks slightly different from the rest of the family. In the later photo, he is the only one going bald. From what Kate said it seems that he was his mother's favourite.

We never knew James, he was badly injured in 1947 after falling out of an apple tree in the orchard opposite Yew Tree Farm. He died three days later having sustained serious internal injuries.

John seemed particularly fond of James when he mentioned him to us, and held a grudge against the tree which he held responsible for his brother's death.

'That blummin' tree,' he muttered, giving it a good kick as we were helping to gather windfalls when I was about eight.

'Why did you do that?' I asked. It was most unlike him to get angry.

'That tree killed my brother!'

'How?' I asked, with the directness of childhood. A question which most adults would have shied away from.

'He was picking apples and he was on his own, see. The ladder slipped and he fell and we weren't near enough to catch him,' explained John. 'He got up and said he was alright, but we sent him back to the farm to lie down, but he never got up again, he was injured and he died three days later.'

'Oh, how awful! Didn't you want to cut that tree

down?' I asked.

'Well, we thought about it, but the apples are good, see, but I don't trust that tree,' replied John, 'it's a bad 'un. We never pick those apples on our own now, we always 'ave someone to 'old the ladder!'

William Reeve

William Reeve was very like his father in appearance. In the family photo he has a droopy moustache which makes him look mournful, but when we knew him he was clean-shaven and quite cheerful.

He was a shy man, but when I was a small child he liked to talk to me over the garden fence as I watched him cut down patches of nettles with a small sickle, on the edge of the orchard behind our garden.

William was very close to his brother John and sister Lizzie. He loved horses and he and John looked after the horses on the farm and later in the First World War. He was in the Royal Garrison Artillery and became a Gunner along with his brother, John, and I think they were put there because they were skilled at dealing with heavy horses. He served four years in France. They never forgot the dreadful suffering endured by the horses in WWI and afterwards had ex-army horses to draw their hay waggons and do other farm work. These horses were always treated with great kindness.

When the First World War broke out, the Reeve family had a conference to decide who should volunteer. They decided that Mr Reeve could not run the farm on his own and in any case farming was important for the war effort. Therefore James and Charles would stay to help run the farm. Ernest, the youngest, was still a schoolboy. William and John the second and fourth sons could be spared from farm work and should volunteer. They joined up and their family never expected them to survive once they realised the seriousness of the war.

Thankfully and luckily, because some luck must have come into it, they both survived. My mother once asked John how they survived, because they fought at Ypres, at Passchendaele and on the Somme, some of the bloodiest battles of World War I. John said that they looked out for each other constantly. William watched him 'like a hawk' and saved his life at least three times, dragging him out of the way of a bullet. He, in his turn watched William and saved his life twice.

I was told that the Simmons family, who lived at Church Farm Little Somerford, never quite forgave the Reeves because they lost their son, Robert, and the Reeves had two sons who survived.

At the start of World War One, the army requisitioned one of the Reeve's carthorses, a black mare called Violet and sadly, they never saw her again.

After World War I, William and John wanted to be more independent, so they rented Union Farm from Wiltshire County Council. Union Farm was at Dauntsey, the next village to Little Somerford, and their favourite sister, Lizzie, was asked to be their housekeeper. They worked very hard and when we visited Union Farm in the 1950s, the farmyard was always neat and clean and freshly swept. In 1958, they retired to *Sunnyside*, a cottage in Little Somerford next to Yew Tree Farm where we got to know them very well.

Charles Reeve

Charles, or more properly Robert Charles Reeve, was a kind man who liked children. This observation is based on several meetings I had with him when I was a small child.

Charles was always well dressed. If we visited the Reeves, Charles would be wearing a beautifully cut tweed jacket and trousers, a shirt and smart waistcoat with a cravat tied at his throat and brown brogue shoes polished to a high gloss.

Once when I was three years old, I went over to Yew Tree Farm with my mother to collect a pint of milk. I was very small for my age and there was some arrangement whereby we bought a daily pint of fresh milk from the farm which I was meant to drink.

I followed my mother up the drive, only to stop in shock and astonishment when I saw a very tall man hobbling in my direction with the aid of two wooden forked sticks which he used to swing himself along. His dark shadow was thrown in front of him by the late afternoon sun and this made him appear to be some giant combination of half insect and half man. I recoiled in terror.

Seeing my horrified expression, he stopped and called out to me: 'Don't be frightened! I just have to use these old sticks because my legs won't work properly. That's all it is!'

I nodded with relief, still staring at his homemade crutches. He asked if we had come to collect the milk and was happy to chat to me until my mother came out of the dairy to see where I had got to.

On another occasion, when I was about five, I was sitting with my mother when she was talking to Kate and Nellie. They had been talking for hours and I was getting restless. I tugged my mother's arm, whereupon I was told off by both my mother and Kate.

Charles, who had been listening in to the conversation, suddenly spoke up in my defence. 'I think she's been very good,' he said, 'You've been nattering for hours and she hasn't had anything to do.'

He looked down at me and winked. Then he turned to the mantlepiece and picked up two small Britains toy dogs which stood there. 'I don't think we have any more use for these,' he said, and to my delight he gave them to me.

Years of constant hard work on the farms had caused severe arthritis in Charles's legs.

Kate described to me years later how Charles had to drive them to the station at Great Somerford so that they could catch the train to Malmesbury when they attended the grammar school. This was before the Malmesbury Branch line was altered to go to Little Somerford station. Charles also drove the milk churns to Dauntsey station every evening so that they could be put on the evening train to London.

Eliza Reeve

Eliza Mary Reeve, or Lizzie, as she was usually called, was more like her brother William in appearance. Lizzie must have had a pleasant personality as all her brothers loved her, especially Ernest, the youngest. He was said to be devoted to Lizzie as she took charge of him soon after he was born and had to get him up, washed and dressed in the mornings. Lizzie was then about fourteen.

Lizzie was an adventurous girl. When a man came to thatch the roof of the kitchen end of Street Farm, he arrived on a large tricyle which he left in one of the cart sheds. Lizzie used to borrow this tricyle and ride it up and down the road until her father found out and stopped her. Lizzie was then about seventeen.

During the First World War Lizzie joined the Red Cross in order to do her bit for the War effort. Her sister Kate described her as being very ladylike.

After WWI, Lizzie was happy to be housekeeper for William and John when they moved to Union Farm, she did not want to have a career like Kate.

We visited the Reeves at Union Farm in 1955 just after Lizzie had been diagnosed with a serious illness. Her doctors gave her just nine weeks to live, but she lived another thirteen years. We were amused to see Lizzie drinking from her invalid cup, which had a spout.

When William, John and Lizzie retired and gave up Union Farm, they moved back to Little Somerford and lived at Sunnyside, the cottage opposite ours when I was five years old.

Lizzie was a very gentle person. I remember going to

visit them one Christmas Eve when I was five. Lizzie was very ill then, but she still thought of me and insisted: 'Give the Little Maid a drink, John.'

John Reeve called her Lina and looked after Lizzie, with tender care when she became ill. On sunny days he helped her out to the porch, where she sat in a wicker chair. Sometimes he would walk her down to the gate so that she might see and talk to any neighbours going by, and I was instructed by my mother to go and chat to them if they were in the garden.

Lizzie died when I was eleven.

Ellen Reeve

Ellen Hester Reeve, known as Nellie was the daughter of Jane Reeve. Although protected by Jane within the family, Nellie felt the stigma, as it was then, of her birth. She was born just a few months before Ernest, the youngest Reeve, so people thought they must be twins, especially as their names began with the same letter and more particularly so as when they asked the other Reeve children if Nellie was their sister, they would say yes, as they had been instructed by their father to always refer to her as, 'My sister, Nellie.'

Poor Nellie was not seen in the village until she was five years old and had to go to school. She was forbidden to be in any of the family photos. Once Mr Reeve had made up his mind about this there was no changing it. Kate once said, 'We did ask Charlie to tell father we didn't mind Nellie being in the family photos, but he wouldn't allow it.'

Nellie had a rather rebellious nature, and would, according to her 'sister' Kate, usually be peering out from behind her bedroom curtains at her family being photographed in the garden below, even though she would be in serious trouble with her grandfather if he found out.

Nellie went to school at Little Somerford. She lived at Street Farm and then later at Yew Tree Farm with Jane, James, Charles and Ernest. Kate was also there in school holidays when she was not away teaching. Kate and Nellie got on very well, both being very strong characters, although they were very different.

Nellie was not afraid to enjoy life and seemed to have made the best of her situation. We knew her when she was in her late fifties. Nellie was the only Reeve to learn to drive and had a series of cars from the 1920s onwards. Each had her own initialled number plate: NHR followed by the number of whichever car it was. The last one was NHR4. She once drove my eldest brother B to Bath hospital when he had appendicitis in 1954.

On the way back from Bath, Nellie stopped to buy some cream cakes in a very expensive shop. My mother thought that was a bit extravagant, but Nellie said, 'I knows what I likes and I *has* what I likes!'

When we first went to Somerford, Nellie had a man friend. He wanted to marry her, but Charles told her 'it was only for her money!' So she did not marry him after all.

Once, when I was five, I had been to visit Kate and

Nellie with my mother. As usual they talked for ages and were still talking as they walked with us down to the garden gate. Suddenly Nellie said; 'Oh, look, Mrs Viner, your husband is looking out to see where you've got to.'

We all turned to look. The head and shoulders of a man was silhouetted at one of the bedroom windows. A light was behind him.

'My husband'll be wanting his tea,' said my mother, 'Come on, Ceri, we must go.' Hastily saying goodbye we hurried across to our house where we found my father sitting by the fire reading. My brothers were out somewhere and had not yet returned.

'You got downstairs quickly,' said my mother.

'What do you mean?' asked my father, 'I've been sitting here all afternoon, I haven't moved.'

'Then *who's upstairs!*' exclaimed my mother. Quickly she explained about the man we had seen at the window. Grabbing the poker my father quietly opened the hall door and told us to get a description if the man ran down the back stairs, or if he jumped out of the window.

My father opened the door to the staircase and went up. He searched everywhere upstairs, including the attic. There was nobody and nobody came down the back stairs as we would have seen them. Nobody jumped out of an upstairs window either as the frames shrieked loudly if they were opened.

That evening, when my brothers came to go to bed, my mother remembered that the boys had broken the light in their room the previous evening when they had a pillow fight, and the bulb had not yet been replaced.

Yet she and I, and Kate and Nellie had all seen a man silhouetted against the window with a light behind him.

Mr Reeve decreed that Nellie was not to be buried in the family plot because people would know that she was illegitimate, even though everyone in the village knew anyway, and though many of the family were dead by the time Nellie died, the surviving siblings would not go against their father's wishes. Nellie is buried in Marlborough and both her mother, Jane and 'sister' Kate chose to be buried next to her.

John Reeve

John Arthur Reeve was a lovely man. Tall and lean, with neat grey hair parted in the middle, he was very kind and was well respected in the village. He always dressed in a striped grandad shirt, waistcoat and trousers, with stout leather shoes. Years of farm work had made him immensely strong and even in his late seventies he would double dig his vegetable patch every spring. He loved horses and was very good with them as he had always looked after the heavy horses on their farm. Educated at Little Somerford School and Malmesbury Grammar he later joined the army and served as a Gunner in the Royal Artillery on the outbreak of war in 1914. He served in France for four years.

As a young man, John Reeve had wanted to marry Ethel Sloper who lived at Fern Cottage then, but as he told us many years later, 'I weren't good enough for 'er.' The Sloper children, Ethel and William had been friends with the Reeves since childhood, but Ethel's mother was ambitious for her children and did not think John was good enough for Ethel, and she refused him. It was a great pity as John never married. Kate remarked to us that Ethel was not nearly good enough for John.

When John and William returned to the village after the First World War they had had a taste of freedom and did not want to work for their father and do what they were told, so they rented Union Farm at Dauntsey and Lizzie went with them to keep house.

John was a very tidy farmer. Hedges were always beautifully cut, ditches dug and the yard swept. Their animals were always looked after with kindness though John was never sentimental and would ring a chicken's neck without hesitation when it was wanted for the pot.

John was very close to his brother, William, and sister, Lizzie, though he did not get on with Kate because she was bossy. He hated it when she tried to tell him what to do. He enjoyed smoking Woodbines and drinking a drop of whisky in the evening, habits of which Kate did not approve.

John tried to keep the peace with Kate by sending us to the shop to buy his cigarettes. He ordered whisky by the crate and would tell us when he was expecting it to be delivered and would ask us not to mention it to his sister.

Later, Kate would say to me:

'Was that the beer lorry I heard stopping at Sunnyside?' Sunnyside was John's cottage.

'I never heard it,' I'd be forced to reply, knowing quite

well the lorry had stopped there.

'Well you must've heard it, you were in the garden; I heard you playing!' Kate glared suspiciously in my direction.

'Yes, but I had to clean my rabbit out! I was at the back,' I'd say hastily, having promised John not to disclose the whisky delivery to Kate.

'Don't tell sister,' he'd say, with a resigned look and then add, 'Dunno what she thinks she's gonna do with all 'er money!'

John looked after Lizzie devotedly when she became ill. Helping her walk, eat and patiently plaiting her hair each day. He disapproved of the modern fashion for short hair and was quite cross with my mother when she insisted on my hair being cut short, even going so far as to offer to plait it for me every morning. Kate Reeve told us that when she had her waist length hair cut into a short bob in the 1920s, John's comment had been: 'Whatever did you have to go and do *that* for!'

John was a keen gardener and would spend long hours in his garden after retirement, mostly either digging or hoeing his vegetable patch or scything the long grass at the edge of the garden. He kept his garden tools in good condition and could often be heard sharpening bill hooks or his scythe, and my mother would send us over with our shears for him to sharpen. He also helped with the harvest and milking at Yew Tree Farm next door.

When we were small, the Reeves still used a carthorse called Captain, and if they were haymaking in Long Ground, the field next to the farm, we would be taken up to watch from the gate. At a convenient point in the work, by prior arrangement, Captain would be unhitched from the hay wain and led over to the gate by John and William Reeve so that we could feed him a carrot or apple before he continued his work.

John Reeve liked children and often talked to us, and he allowed us to help with small jobs such as picking up windfall apples in the orchard behind our house. He would tell us about the trees and the old apple varieties and how they once picked nineteen bushels of apples off the big apple tree in our hedge when he was a boy. (A bushel of apples is forty-six pounds in weight and about the size of one of those large wicker log baskets).

When I was seven years old, I wandered over to Yew Tree Farm to watch the haymaking in Long Ground, a field near the farm. John and William Reeve were turning the hay by hand with long wooden rakes. I wanted to help and picked up a spare rake which was so long and heavy I could hardly lift it. I struggled to turn the hay for ten minutes and looking around I suddenly realised I was on my own, William had gone back to the farm to start the milking and now John had disappeared too. Suddenly I saw John returning with a very small wooden rake, a child sized one. He had gone back to get it so that I could help. This small rake must have been specially made for the Reeve children when they were small. I never forgot his kindness.

On one occasion when I was nine, John Reeve was going down to the cemetery to tidy the family graves and he allowed me to accompany him once I had permission from my mother and had promised to behave myself. He showed me the graves of his parents and three older brothers, and after hoeing the weeds from around the graves he remarked: 'That's where I'm gonna be.'

He pointed with his hoe to a space next to the grave of his brother, William, who had died the year before. 'Well, either there or just a bit further along, depending on who goes first.'

I was very sorry when John Reeve died, but comforted by the thought that in death he was surrounded by his family.

Kate Reeve

I knew Kate Annie Reeve particularly well and visited her at least once a week so she told me all about our village and many memories she had.

When Kate was about three years old, her brother James, then aged twenty-two, carried her on his shoulders out to Little Orchard to show her a dead fox. 'Poor pussy,' she said.

Kate went to the village school when she was six years old. She was said to be 'sharp as a needle'. The youngest children sat on stools, but the older children had to stand up for a lot of the time or sit cross-legged on the floor. The older children stood back-to-back so that they should not copy each other. They all had slates to write on to begin with. They did arithmetic and composition. The boys did drawing and the girls sewed nightdresses! There were six standards, Standard 1 being the bottom one. Miss Croombe took nature study with the lower class. History and Geography were also taught. The pupils had to memorise the names of places and rivers, and kings and queens.

On one occasion, some men visited Mr Reeve to discuss the railway going over his land. They saw some primroses in a vase in the sitting room and asked if they could have them. Mr Reeve called Kate in to ask her permission for the men to take the flowers as she had picked them.

Once when Kate was a girl, the front door was varnished and Kate accidentally smudged it when it was wet. Fearful of being punished for this, Kate hid in one of the sheds.

At Christmas time a man used to come round playing a concertina and Kate remembered being brought down in her night gown to hear him play.

Kate and her sisters used to visit the Sloper family who lived at Fern Cottage (called The Cottage in those days). They used to go upstairs to talk to old Mrs Sloper who used to sit in her rocking chair knitting and minding the baby.

There was a laundry then at East End Farm, at the top of East End Lane, run by two old ladies. Kate used to take the dirty collars up on Monday evenings and collect them on Saturdays so that the men in the family would have clean collars for church on Sundays. A woman in the village helped with the other family washing. There was a donkey feeding on the verge which belonged to John Day, who lived at Sunnyside then. Kate was afraid of the donkey.

At harvest time she used to ride on the hay cart back to the farm. At that time they had two horses, Flower and Violet. Violet was black and Flower was creamy brown in colour.

Kate left the village school at fourteen and after several months she went to Malmesbury Grammar School. She caught the train from Great Somerford as the Malmesbury branch line went to Great Somerford then. Her brothers took her down in the pony trap if the weather was wet, but she had to walk back in the evening. The train got to Malmesbury at 8.40am. School finished at 4.30pm and the train left at 4.50pm – a ticket for three months cost nineteen shillings and sixpence.

Other young people from the village who caught the train included Bob, Nancy and Fred Simmons from Church Farm, Willy Sloper from Fern Cottage next to Street Farm, and Ray and Edgar Ody, who lived at Idover Farm on the Dauntsey Road. The Odys were rather large boys and were known as *Big Pudding* and *Little Pudding.*

Ray once remarked, 'I shouldn't marry you, Kate – you wouldn't give me enough to eat!'

Kate had religious instruction lessons from the vicar, Rev. Browne, together with Phyllis Ponting, who lived at the level crossing cottage in Mill Lane, Nancy Simmons from Church Farm and Ethel Sloper from Fern Cottage.

When Kate was thirteen, Mrs Reeve asked the postmaster which was best for Kate, working in the post office or being a teacher? They decided that teaching would be better, so from the age of fourteen to sixteen

Kate became a pupil-teacher at Little Somerford school, teaching at the school during alternate weeks and spending every second week as a pupil at Malmesbury Grammar School. She had a free railway ticket to school from the county and free schooling. Whether this was the normal provision for pupil teachers I do not know. It cost four pounds ten shillings a term in those days to go to Malmesbury Grammar School.

When there was anything on at the Grammar school, Bob Simmons used to bring Kate back from school in a governess cart. Her pay for being a pupil-teacher was twelve pounds for the first year, fourteen pounds for the second year and sixteen pounds for the third year. She paid her mother about eight pounds towards her keep, but she was allowed to keep the rest of her money. This must have caused some resentment among her brothers and sisters who worked just as hard, but never had any money of their own.

Kate's first job was at Clyffe Pypard First School and her brother, Charles, drove her over in the trap for her interview with Canon Goddard. She stayed at Clyffe Pypard during the week, cycled home on Friday nights and cycled back on Monday morning. If it was raining she would be driven back by Charles. She was teaching at Clyffe Pypard for three years, after which she moved to Castle Eaton where she was in digs with a Miss Long who was the headmistress. She was there during the serious influenza epidemic of 1918. Kate had a bad attack of influenza, but survived. She was sad to learn that one of her pupils had died from the infection.

Kate moved to a school in Marlborough after a few years. While she was there she became friendly with a married man and when her brother Charles got to hear about it he insisted she leave her job so she moved to Tisbury and after a couple of years applied to be headmistress of a school in Limmington, near Yeovil in Somerset (c1930). She was very happy there and stayed for twenty-four years until she retired.

Kate came back to Little Somerford during the holidays and this caused some resentment amongst her brothers and sisters who never had holidays and were not given any wages either, so there was some talk of Kate being excluded from inheriting the family farm as she never did any work on it and expected to have a rest during the school holidays. In fact, Kate outlived all her brothers and sisters and inherited the farm, though I think it must have been very sad to be the last surviving sibling and to know that the whole family had died off.

Yew Tree Farm was very old-fashioned. The sink and old water pump were outside the back door under a covered area. Cooking was done on the old range until the house was partly modernised in 1958 when a sink with hot and cold water was put in and the old range bricked over and a modern range installed. Ernest was still expected to use the old sink outside to wash his hands after work.

Kate had a pleasant side to her and enjoyed chatting about the village, but unfortunately she was very abrupt in her manner, especially if she did not know people well. Maybe she was shy, but she was certainly difficult to get to know. Therefore many people in the village avoided her because they were wary of her brusque manner.

She certainly had a lot of courage. Once when she was crippled with arthritis I took her out in her wheelchair. Feeling unusually sorry for herself she said: 'I used to walk over those fields, but I haven't been able to go over them for years now.'

'Well, what's stopping you?' I retorted. 'You've got your chair and I can push you. You can go over them anytime you like.'

Kate stared at me. 'Do you really think so?'

'Why not?' I said, 'You can do anything if you really want to.'

So a few days later when the weather was fine and dry, we set off. I pushed her wheelchair halfway up Clay Street to the wooden gate into Strange's Croft. Opening the gate I pushed her through into the field and after closing the gate behind us we set off.

Luckily the grass was quite short, the cows had recently been in the field cropping the grass, and carefully avoiding any cow pats we made steady progress, Kate commenting on the view and the quality of the grass as we passed.

We were fine until we reached the second gateway. The wheelchair was heavy to push and I had not bargained for the fact that the gateway was very muddy, having been trodden into ruts by the cows as they pushed their way through. We got stuck in a muddy puddle. Cursing myself for having come that way I struggled to lift the wheelchair clear. Luckily, David Gleed, the farm man, had seen us and came to our rescue.

Between us we lifted the wheelchair away from the muddy gateway and onto firm ground and then it was an easy journey back to the farm. Although relieved to be back home safely, Kate was evidently very pleased that we had gone over the fields and it cheered her up immensely.

However, Kate was mean and penny-pinching in her ways, to the extent that she would buy two types of cake for tea, one better quality one for herself and any guests and another, the cheapest one she could find, usually a Jamaica Ginger Cake, for David Gleed who worked on the farm and came in for a cup of tea and slice of cake every day.

'When she goes,' he'd mutter, 'I'm never eatin' this sort've cake again!

She would also eat food that not only had gone off, but was green with mould.

'You're surely not going to eat *that!'* we would say to her.

'Oh, yes, that'll just do me,' she'd say.

'You can't eat it, it's bad!' we'd argue, 'It'll make you ill. Throw it away!" but to no avail.

'Waste not, want not,' she'd say. This had been dinned into her as a little girl and no-one could change her outlook.

She loved to reminisce about her childhood and teaching days and to hear gossip about the villagers. When told a salacious piece of gossip, she would slap her thigh and exclaim: 'Oh, my patience!'

Ernest Walter Reeve

'Poor old Ernie!' was usually the comment when Ernest was mentioned when we were growing up. Everyone who knew him felt sorry for him because his whole life was one of unremitting hard work. He seemed to have nothing in his life other than work.

Ernest Walter Reeve was the youngest of the Reeves and was probably the most affected by Nellie's birth as they were born just a few months apart. People assumed that Ernest and Ellen must be twins, especially since the Reeve children all said that Nellie was their sister.

In the family photo of 1914, Ernest is the very handsome lad sitting on a rug in front of his parents.

Ernest attended the village school and then his father paid for him to attend Malmesbury Grammar School like his brothers. He was thirteen when World War I started and when he was seventeen he tried to join up, but, as he later told me, he was rejected because he was short sighted.

Ernest never got away to live a life of his own. He worked on the farm all his life and hardly ever had a day off. He was known as '*The Boy*' by his older brothers even when he was in his sixties. 'Have you seen the Boy?' John Reeve would enquire.

'Do you mean my brothers?' I replied.

'No, I mean The Boy,' said John. 'Ah, there 'e is!' and waving his stick to catch Ernie's attention, John hurried to catch him up.

Ernest once told me that he had had the opportunity to buy Street Farm in the 1940s but he had not done so and he later wished he had. I think this was because Ernest lacked confidence.

When I was very small the Reeve brothers looked alike to me as they all dressed the same way in striped, collarless grand-dad shirts, waistcoats, corduroy trousers tied at the ankles, and flat caps. They were tall and wiry in build, though Will was a little shorter than the others, and Ernest fitted this description as well as any of them.

I first became aware of Ernie as an individual when he gave us a lift on the hay wain.

My father had taken M aged six, and myself, aged five, to Malmesbury. We probably needed new shoes because we did not normally go with him. We caught the bus back which happened to be the Swindon bus which did not go through the village, but stopped at the top of Little Somerford Hill. We got off the bus and had just walked around the corner when our father called to us to keep in as the hay wain was coming. Drawn by Captain the carthorse whom we greatly admired, the great hay wain came slowly round the corner dipping and swaying as Captain negotiated the sharp turn. Its woodwork was painted red with *Reeve Bros. Little Somerford* in blue lettering along the back. Ernest was driving it and much to our surprise he stopped and offered us a lift down The Hill.

After checking with Ernest that our weight would not be too much for the horse. My father seized each of us in turn, and climbing up the wooden rack at the back of the cart he placed us on the hay, telling us to sit very still and hold on to one of the ropes holding the load together. Then he climbed up behind us and held on to us as the wain set off. I shall never forget that wonderful ride, the hay wain creaking and swaying on its journey down The Hill, the soft sweet-smelling hay beneath us. We must have been some of the last children in England to have the pleasure of that experience as most farmers used tractors then, but the Reeves had been born in Victorian times. They had used horses all their lives and they kept the old tradition until 1958.

At the bottom of The Hill we turned along our road and the hay wain stopped outside our house. We were lifted down and shouted out our thanks before watching the laden waggon turn into the farm drive at Yew Tree Farm, just past our house.

I was then able to distinguish Ernest from his brothers when we saw him cutting hedges or driving a waggon. We did not get to talk to him until we were older. Like his brothers he was very kind to us. Once when I was sent by my brothers to ask for some bailer twine which we wanted for a rope ladder, Ernest gave me a great armful of it.

'Is this enough?' he asked. 'Come and ask if you need any more,' he added.

When I was ten I got to know him a bit better as I was asked to call at Yew Tree Farm and collect any letters Kate might have. These I would take to the post, whereupon I had to report back to say they had been posted and I would be given a toffee.

On some occasions I found Ernest in the yard feeding the pigs and he let me stir the pig swill in the bucket and then watch the pigs guzzling their meal as he poured it into the trough. Sometimes he would tell me about the latest calf or about the vet's visit to de-horn the cows.

Ernest was very fond of the farm animals. On one occasion he was very sad when he saw me looking over the door of Captain's old stable. The horse's headcollar and harness still hung in the corner. 'We 'aven't got a horse any more. I sold 'im a few years ago and he died soon after. I think he died of a broken heart; I wish I 'adn't sold 'im,' he said sadly.

Ernest was a shy man with a rather high voice. If he was told some village news which was not good he would say: 'Baaaaad Joooob,' (Bad Job) in a mournful voice, drawing the words out so that he sounded rather like a bleating goat. This amused us so much that this phrase has gone down in family history and my brothers and I still use it today.

Unfortunately, when his older brothers died, Ernest was left alone at Yew Tree with his very bossy sister Kate. In a most uncharacteristic comment for a man who was normally kind and even tempered, he muttered bitterly to my mother: ' I'd rather 'twere any of 'em, *any* of 'em, but 'er!'

On one occasion Ernest had to go to hospital for some tests. It was July. He must have enjoyed having a lie-in because when my mother visited him he remarked: 'It's to be hoped I'm here for Christmas!'

Kate took over all the farm accounts and although Ernest was the joint owner of the farm you would never have guessed it from the way Kate treated him. He never had any wages or any other money of his own. When he went to the weekly market at Devizes, Kate would give him a shilling so that he could buy half a pint of beer. All the other farmers felt sorry for him and would always buy him a pint. Ernie used to hide a few coppers and one or two toffees, away in the loft above the stable. 'Don't tell sister,' he'd say.

Once when my mother and I were visiting them one evening, my mother offered to make them a drink and asked Ernie if he'd like beer or coffee. 'Coffee, please,' he replied.

'Oh Ernest!' bullied Kate, 'You know you always have beer!'

My mother protested that coffee would be no trouble to make, but Kate wouldn't hear of it.

In the evenings when we visited them, Ernie would sit in the kitchen and when it grew dark he would switch the light on, whereupon Kate would call from the other room: 'Ernest, are you reading?'

'Noooo' came the bleating reply.

'Are you watching television?' said Kate, knowing perfectly well that the television was in the living room and switched off.

'Noooo'

'Then put that light out!' scalded Kate, who was sitting in the well lit living room. Poor Ernest would have to spend the rest of the evening sitting in the dark.

Until after 1960, Ernest rode a bicycle which had solid tyres; it had been purchased in 1921! For a bicycle lamp he used a small 'bulls eye' lamp with a stub of candle in. Then his bicycle became so rusty that it was decided that he really ought to have a new one and Ernest was very pleased to have a more comfortable bicycle with soft tyres. It was probably the only new thing he had had in the previous fifty years! Kate would never have allowed him to buy new clothes when they had all the clothes left by Charles, William and John.

One thing I shall never forget is the sound of Ernie calling the cows in for milking, a long, yodelling call which we heard every summer for years during our childhood. We really missed this sound when Ernie died.

I saw Ernie's ghost on the morning he died. When I was a teenager I used to go over to Yew Tree Farm and do a few jobs in the house on a Sunday morning. Then I would lay the table and take the joint out of the oven. Kate and Ernest were both crippled with arthritis then and could put the joint in the oven but could not take it out, when it was very hot, as they walked with crutches and so couldn't use both hands at once.

When the lunch was ready I walked into the sitting room to help Ernest up from his chair. I handed him his crutches and walked beside him, opening doors for him as he hobbled slowly through the hall and sitting room into the kitchen at the back of the house. He sat down at the table. Saying goodbye, I left them to eat their lunch and walked back through the sitting room, into the hall and out of the front door. As I shut the front door I glanced at the sitting room window and to my horror I saw Ernie standing there in his usual clothes and with his flat cap on his head, but instead of his face I saw a skull!

I knew immediately that Ernest was going to die.

A few minutes later we were sitting down to our own lunch when Mrs Dolly Isles, a neighbour, knocked on our door to tell us that Ernie had died as he ate his dinner, just two minutes after I left the house. He had never moved from his chair in the kitchen.

I was horrified to hear from a neighbour afterwards that as Ernie's dead body was slumped in his chair, Kate, having sat opposite her brother's body to eat her lunch, gobbled up what was left of Ernie's saying: 'Can't waste that!'

CHAPTER 21

SNOW (THE BIG FREEZE OF 1962–3)

'Snowing!' exclaimed M, 'I told you it would.'

I leapt up from my chair and pressed my nose against the cold glass of the window and squinted out. Dense, heavy snowflakes showed pale against the dark. Already there was an inch of snow on the path, obliterating and smoothing out the uneven stones.

We rushed through the draughty lobby to the living room to announce this exciting news to our parents who were having a cup of tea. Our father, muttering gloomily that we were 'in for it and had better get some paraffin in as soon as the garage opened' went out to the cold scullery to set a lamp under the sink to prevent the pipe freezing.

We had used the end room over Christmas and although it was only Boxing Day we were told to stay in the living room to conserve fuel so that the open fire in the end room could be let out and our small stock of wood saved for emergencies.

When we woke up the next morning it was still

snowing hard. At least nine inches of snow had fallen overnight and there was no sign of it stopping. There was no heating upstairs and the cold was intense. Ferny leaves of ice coated the windows on the inside of the glass, creating a beautiful pattern that no modern etched glass could equal. We breathed on a small patch, our breath clouding in the cold air, until we made a small spy hole. There was such a blizzard that you could barely see your hand if you held it in front of your eyes. My father went out to clear the path to the gate, and then prepared to walk the three and a half miles to Malmesbury to get a supply of food in. My mother made a list of essentials.

'Put the kettle on, Ceri,' she ordered, 'and help me make sandwiches.'

The heavy wooden sledge was brought out, and armed with a shovel, a flask of tea and some sandwiches, my father set off. He returned eight hours later, looking like a Yeti, snow clinging to his duffle coat, his beard and his eyebrows. Cold and exhausted, he described having to dig through deep drifts along the main road.

The blizzard was so bad that we were not even allowed out until it stopped. Very heavy snow continued to fall for three days and nights. On the fourth day we woke up to a changed world. The clouds had cleared and the white blanketed garden dazzled the eye. Flocks of hungry birds huddled in the trees, their feathers puffed up to protect them from the cold. Scraps of bread and a bowl of water were put out on our bird table and replenished at regular intervals and we spent a lot of time watching the birds squabbling over these.

The garden was now an unfamiliar landscape of gentle white undulations. Tree branches were highlighted in white; the box bush had become a large, white dumpling. This snow was not the usual two or three inches which turned to mushy slush in the middle of the day, but was proper snow, perfect for snowmen, sledging and snowballs.

Wrapped up in coats and gloves, we rushed into this changed world, hurling snowballs at each other. As usual I ended up with snow down my neck! There was sledging on Old Cousins, a sloping field on the side of The Hill opposite the pub and we joined three or four other groups of children to take our turns. Some of the younger adults came out too, one of them skiing down the slope. At regular intervals we returned home to thaw out our frozen hands and dry our sodden gloves on the top of the paraffin heater. I was sent to check on two elderly neighbours to see if they needed anything from the shop, and to inform them which foodstuffs might be shared if supplies in the village shop ran out. We trudged to the garage to get gallons of paraffin for our heater; supplies were rationed after a few days.

Sometimes the children would gang together and roll huge snowballs over three feet high. Giant snowmen adorned verges and gardens

The weather established a pattern of clear cold days, clouding over in late afternoon and snowing heavily at night. Nobody could get out of the village as snow ploughs were busy elsewhere. Our days were spent doing only essential jobs as we only had one room which was heated. Washing was hung out, but froze solid on the line. Starving birds were fed with scraps and armfuls of hay were put in our rabbit's hutch which was in a shed outside. Luckily we had a few sprouts and winter greens growing in the garden. These were targeted by hungry pigeons, their feathers puffed up out of all recognition by the cold. These poor creatures grew so hungry that they were almost tame and John Reeve, our elderly neighbour, caught several pigeons to eat. We were given some, but after such a prolonged cold spell there was not much meat on them.

It snowed each night and froze hard and then snowed and froze again. The snow was so deep in the fields that even the hedges were covered and you could walk over them as the snow had frozen in a solid crust. Only the rows of elms, their branches glittering against the duck egg blue sky, indicated where they were. In the middle of the day there was a slight thaw. Icicles hung from the roofs and some of these icy daggers were over a foot long and we were warned not to stand underneath them. We broke some off a low doorway and licked them like ice lollies. They tasted mossy and slightly earthy and we soon abandoned this experiment.

The village school was open as the headmistress lived next door, and in the new year I reluctantly returned to school, but my brothers who attended Malmesbury Grammar, stayed at home as there were twenty-five foot snowdrifts along the main road. If there was heavy snow we were sent home early as some children had a long walk home.

It was three weeks before the snow plough forged its way along the top road and down The Hill. Piles of snow were heaped along the verges, making handy ammunition for impromptu snowball fights.

The cold continued week after week; snow showers were less frequent, but there was no thaw until early March when ice filled ditches turned to water again and patches of flattened grass showed along the hedge banks. Eventually green verges appeared still decorated with giant snowballs, until even these thawed to unidentifiable lumps of ice. The big freeze was over and spring was more than welcome that year.

CHAPTER 22

JUMBLE SALES

Jumble sales were held about four times a year in the Village Hall, a large wooden hut painted cream and brown on the outside and with varnished wood on the inside, which stood on the corner of Mill Lane.

The jumble sales were held to raise funds for the church or some village activity such as the Over-Sixties' Outing. There were some well off families in the village which meant that some of the jumble was very good quality, so the sales were eagerly anticipated and well attended, not only by many people from our village, but by others from Great Somerford, Brinkworth and Dauntsey.

Stall holders collected items for weeks beforehand and every family was expected to contribute something. Once I was twelve, I was asked to help set up the stalls. First, the long, heavy wooden trestle tables had to be hauled out of their cobwebby cupboard where they were stored, and carried into the main hall. They were set up around the edge of the room. Stalls included clothes, shoes, toys, books, bric-a-brac, refreshments and a raffle.

There was such a demand for clothes that they were sorted beforehand into men's, women's and children's garments, and then into piles of similar garments such as trousers, dresses or skirts. Anything really good was put aside and offered to particular villagers who had mentioned beforehand that they were looking for a school blazer for their child or a pretty dress.

Half an hour beforehand the sale queues began to form as impatient customers waited for the doors to be opened. Once the bolts were drawn back a great crowd of people surged into the room, anxious to grab a bargain. Having paid their sixpences at the door, they rushed to the clothes stalls and began grabbing armfuls of garments. Any slower customers were likely to see articles snatched from under their noses and occasionally from their hands.

On one occasion, Stella Barnes, a friend's mother beckoned me over.

'Here, Ceri, this is a really good suit. It's Chanel,' she said, holding up a vivid pink jacket with gilt buttons and a matching skirt. 'It'll just do you. It's a shame my Julie's too big for it, otherwise I'd have it for her! It's a shilling.'

She continued, 'Don't worry now, yer mum can pay me next week. I'll keep it for you. Don't forget to come and collect it before you go, otherwise it'll be gone! By the way, there's an iron mark on the skirt.' She pointed out a nasty brown mark where the skirt had been carelessly ironed, 'but that don't matter, a bit've lemon juice'll get that off!'

The brown iron mark was obviously why the suit was

in the sale. Stella was right and a careful rub with half a lemon, and a sponge with a clean wet cloth removed the stain entirely. I ended up with a beautiful suit worn for years by both myself and my mother.

I usually only had sixpence to spend at jumble sales, so unless I needed school uniform, I would browse the bric-a-brac and oddments. I was once lucky to find a belt with a lovely black buckle on each end which hooked together to make a diamond shape when worn. I bought it for sixpence and took it home. My father advised me to polish the buckle as he thought it might be silver, which it was. Many years later I sold the buckle for a substantial profit on my initial sixpence.

If I was helping, I was usually given a toasted teacake and a cup of tea at the refreshment stall. The refreshments were popular and a team of ladies were kept very busy, pouring tea, buttering scones and toasting teacakes.

Groups of children made for the toy stall where some discovered their old toys which their mothers had turned out and bought them back. There were brisk sales of toy farm animals at one penny and Dinky toys at threepence. The children would then rush to their parents to show off their purchases and beg for a few more pennies to spend. Sometimes they would be hauled away from the toy stall and made to try on some clothes!

On the corner of the refreshment stall there was often a competition such as: *Guess the number of sweets in a jar,* or *Guess the weight of the fruit cake.* People paid sixpence to enter the competition and the nearest correct guess won the prize. The noise in the hall was tremendous, as once having made their purchases, many people wanted to exchange gossip over a cup of tea and a slice of Victoria sponge or a buttered scone.

At last the restless hubbub settled down to a calmer tone as the best items were sold. Stalls were tidied and the clothes that were left re-sorted. Some were put aside for the school dressing-up box, others were donated to needy families and a few were put away for the next sale, but usually there was not much left.

Someone on the parish council would call for silence while the raffle was drawn and the winners announced. While they had everyone's attention they would thank the organisers and stallholders, to heartfelt clapping and cheers. This also ensured that the hardworking team of organisers would help on future occasions.

At one sale there was an extra appeal for a lady's handbag, complete with purse and lipstick which had been sold by accident when she was helping on the clothes stall. She had been unwise enough to put it down on a chair next to the stall. Thankfully, the bag was handed over and the lady refunded the money she had paid. My friend was very indignant that her beautiful soft leather handbag had been sold for only nine pence!

After that came the clearing up. Stallholders rapidly cleared up, triumphant buyers left carrying bulging carrier bags. A clattering of dishes in the kitchen indicated that several ladies were washing up. The takings were counted. Tables were folded and returned to their cupboard. The floor was swept and rubbish collected. Finally the volunteers headed home, pleased with a job well done, and the hall was locked until the next event.

Postscript

The lady who had donated the Chanel suit saw me wearing it a week later, and after inspecting me closely she demanded angrily to know how the stain had been removed. She was obviously very cross at having parted with a favourite item of dress, but I thought it was rather amusing. I wish I had the suit today, my mother gave it away.

CHAPTER 23

THE VILLAGE FETE

The fete was the most important event of the village year. Together with its winter counterpart the Christmas Bazaar, it raised funds for our church of St John the Baptist. It was always held in mid-July and usually at Manor Farm, the home of Colonel and Mrs Brassey (later Sir Hugh and Lady Brassey).

The beautifully manicured lawn was covered with stalls: Tombola, Plant, Cake and Bottle stalls, a Treasure Hunt pitch and a Lucky Dip for the children and of course a raffle. Bales of hay at one side marked the bowling area and another roped off area was used for the children's fancy dress and later, the dog show. Everybody in the village assisted or contributed raffle prizes or cakes, plants or bottles. There were endless opportunities for spending money and people came from all the surrounding villages for a good day out.

First there would be a welcome by the Vicar and a round of applause for the generous hosts whose lawn was being ruined in aid of church funds. A few words would be said and a ribbon cut by a local celebrity before crowds of people surged forwards, anxious to buy the best cake on the cake stall, or in hopes of winning a worthwhile prize on the tombola or bottle stall. My favourite stall was the spinning Jenny, an octagonal-shaped table divided into numbered segments of equal size. A large wooden arrow was fixed to a central spindle so it could be spun freely. Small prizes would be laid out and people placed their sixpence on their chosen segment. The arrow was spun and everyone watched in fascination to see where it would stop. Eventually it wobbled to a standstill and the lucky winner took their prize while the stallholder hastily gathered a handful of sixpences from the table before inviting more onlookers to try their luck. I once won a tiny Murano glass vase on this and I still have it nearly sixty years later.

The bottle stall was extremely popular as prizes included bottles of wine, sherry and whisky, so sales of tickets were brisk. There was a tombola stall where people could pay six pence for three small wooden hoops which they had to throw over a prize to win. Children queued for the Lucky Dip, small wrapped toys hidden in a tub of sawdust. Then a voice over the loudspeaker would announce the children's fancy dress and mothers would help their children into costumes and masks. Then spacemen, mermaids and characters from children's stories would parade round a small ring. Proud parents would take photographs and after conferring, the judges would announce the winners to loud applause. Prizes would be presented by the local celebrity who had opened the fete and a photographer from the local paper would be there to record the occasion.

A small piglet in a pen of hay bales was the recipient of much admiration throughout the day. This was the prize for the bowling champion. The bowling took place in a series of closely contested heats with the finals in the afternoon. The proud winner was later seen wheeling their piglet home in a wheelbarrow!

Also in the afternoon was the dog show, with agility and obedience classes which seemed to be as much for the owners as for the dogs. Then came the more amusing classes: *The Most Handsome Animal* was a subject of great discussion. *The Dog Most Like Its Owner* caused much laugher and comment, but most amusing of all was the *Dog Fancy Dress.* I can still remember a small, yappy Norfolk terrier called Wattie dressed as a Red Indian, wearing a small headdress of feathers and with a miniature bow and quiver of arrows fixed to a belt round its midriff. Another dog, a tall rangy mongrel, was dressed as *King of the Road* after a famous pop song of the day. The dog sported a stick stuck through its collar and pointing over its shoulder. At the end of the stick was a large pork chop protruding from a red spotted handkerchief. Much hilarity was provoked as the dog tried to get at the pork chop as its owner tried to haul it round the ring in front of the judges.

The tea tent, run by a team of busy village ladies provided refreshment throughout the day. Morning coffee and cakes were followed by light lunches and later, cream teas with fresh scones and jam, strawberries and cream, or Victoria sponges or fruit cake and endless cups of tea.

Then, about five o'clock, stallholders started to clear up. Crowds thinned out as people began to depart, many clutching their purchases or winnings. Litter was collected up, money counted and stalls dismantled. Eventually only patches of trampled grass and a few small holes indicated that another successful fete was over.

CHAPTER 24

FIRE ON THE RAILWAY

One Summer afternoon there was a loud knock on the door and a neighbour asking urgently for my father's help. A spark from a passing steam engine had set fire to dried grass on the railway embankment and the fire was spreading quickly. Immediate action was needed to prevent the fire destroying growing crops nearby. The fields affected by the fire were part of East End Farm.

My mother and I looked out of the living room window and could see small drifts of smoke in the distance. My father hurried off to help and my mother asked me to assist in making sandwiches for the firefighters while she made two thermos flasks of tea. Taking an old blanket to sit on, we set off up East End Lane with the refreshments. Just a little way up the lane we turned off through the open field gate to where several villagers were standing apprehensively watching the fire and deciding how best to help. The fire had begun to spread rapidly since the ground was very dry after a spell of warm weather.

A pile of hessian sacks and several buckets of water had been quickly supplied by the Reeves at Yew Tree Farm, the nearest farm to the blaze. The sacks were soaked in water and handed to any available village men who had come to help. Two men dashed off to neighbouring farms to beg for more sacks, while others made a chain to bring buckets of water from the farm. People made suggestions as to who else might be available to help fight the fire, such as local farm workers, gardeners or retired men who were still able bodied. Somebody with a bicycle was sent to seek them out. More village men began to arrive and somebody dashed up with another armful of sacks. The fire brigade had been summoned, but the nearest engine was already out on a job, so we would have to wait for one to come from further away. A line of volunteers could be seen wielding the sacks like flails to smother the creeping flames. The fire had spread down the embankment to the field and so needed to be fought on several flanks.

Firefighting was thirsty work. Every twenty minutes or so, men, their faces and arms streaked and blackened by ash and their shirts stained with sweat and grime, would dash over to their wives and thankfully gulp down a beaker of tea or squash before hurrying back to their task. The village women were sitting on blankets anxiously watching the progress of their menfolk and dealing out cups of tea or orange squash. Thankfully there were over a dozen men helping. Some were on the field itself, where the fire had encroached, others were on the steep railway embankment. There was a water tank beside the railway line here and trains stopped to take on water. It was thought that this was most likely when a spark from a boiler had ignited the dry vegetation on the side of the line. Everybody was relieved when a fire engine turned into the field. The firemen could access the water in the tank by the line and soon set about thoroughly soaking not only the burnt area, but the dried grass next to it so that the fire was prevented from spreading. Clouds of steam rose into the air as the water hit the glowing embers.

Now that everyone knew that the fire was under control and almost out, a picnic atmosphere developed and the exhausted village men were happy to take turns to sit on the grass for a few minutes and enjoy sandwiches and cake while chatting to their friends before returning to the fray.

At last, after several hours of hard work, the fire was out, although smoke and steam still drifted upwards from the charred ground. People gathered up the litter and empty flasks and set off home. The firemen remained for some time damping down the area.

CHAPTER 25

SOMERFORD SHOW

Somerford Show was always a highlight of our summer holiday because it was not only a produce show, but also included hobby and handicraft sections which were especially for children. Entries were submitted for a small fee and this money was redistributed to the lucky prize winners. A first prize of two shillings and six pence, the old half-crown, was much sought after, but the second and third prizes of one shilling and six pence, and one shilling respectively, were not to be sneezed at by children desirous of extra pocket money.

A programme was obtained by our mother and much discussion took place as to which classes we could enter. Classes included: *a Scrap Book, an Animal Carved from a Vegetable, a Hand-painted Jam Jar, a Painting on a Given Subject, a Vase of Wild Flowers, a Photograph with a Caption, and an Item of Handicraft.*

I usually entered a scrap book, an animal carved from a vegetable and a hand painted jam jar. B liked to enter a photograph and sometimes M entered a painted jam jar and a vase of wildflowers. If I had made a gingham apron at school, I was able to enter this. The aprons had nine rows of cross stitch on both the bottom half and the bib and much concentration and wincing over pricked fingers had gone into their production. On another occasion I had success with a picture composed of felt pieces sewn onto a linen background. One of these was a haymaking scene which I still have.

There were adult classes too, many of which included beautifully matched and arranged home grown vegetables such as onions, runner beans and tomatoes. Prizes and local recognition for top quality fruit or sponge cakes, jams, chutneys and supper dishes were much sought after by the local ladies. The standard was extremely high. There were also adult handicraft classes such as hand knitted jumpers, photographs, paintings and *Something New from Something Old.*

My mother once won first prize for a rag rug made from a hessian sack which had once held cow cake. The words: Wiltshire Farmers were printed on it. Once it was cut open and spread out, it made a good base for a rag rug made from strips of our old clothes hand knotted into it with a latch hook.

One problem I had was finding enough material for my scrap book, so I usually asked Kate Reeve, our neighbour at Yew Tree Farm. She produced a pile of old Bibby's Farming Calendars. Bibby's was a cattle food firm, alas now long taken over. These calendars had the most beautiful pictures of farm animals, and these together with a few old birthday and Christmas cards and one or two magazines were enough for me to get to work. My scrap books were a great success and I won prizes for them on three successive years, after which I was too old to enter. On one occasion I spent all day before the show carefully painting butterflies onto my chosen jam jar, and then painted the inside of it a creamy yellow to show them up. When I went into the marquee on show day, one lady insisted to me that they were transfers, even though they were not.

The show was held in Major Sturgis's field next to Great Somerford Rectory and just within the Little Somerford village boundary, about a mile and a quarter from Somerford corner. On the day of the show, entries were taken carefully into the large marquee and laid as attractively as possible into their allotted spaces. Prizes were never guaranteed as the standard of entries was high. Each item was given a number so that the entries were anonymous. Then came the long wait while the judging took place, after which everyone rushed in to see if their entries had won and to exclaim about the justice of the prize awards. The items could not be removed until five o'clock so we usually went home and came back in the evening for the other highlight of the day, the funfair.

In the daytime the rides did not look very exciting, but by dusk, when the throbbing music had started up and strings of coloured lights illuminated each ride or stall; when the air was thick with the suppressed excitement of the children, the calls of the ride owners, the smell of hot dogs, fried onions and candy floss – that was another matter entirely.

There was a carousel with gallopers which I particularly

liked, also a switchback, dodgems, a rifle range, coconut shy, swing boats and a stall where you had to throw three ping pong balls into bowls in order to win a goldfish. My mother was particularly good at this and on at least three occasions we went home with a goldfish in a plastic bag full of water. The fish was usually given to M who was a keen fisherman. One goldfish was named Elmer and lived for over eleven years. We were only allowed on one or two rides as money was limited, so we normally went on the switchback and M and I shared a dodgem car while B tried to win a coconut on the coconut shy. He was often successful so he obviously inherited our mother's skill at throwing.

Then it was time to go home, the loud music of the fair blasting out from the loudspeaker, the excited screams of the girls on the dodgems, the smell of hot dogs and candy floss overpowering the grassy smell of the Wiltshire field. The music gradually faded as we trudged back up the road to our village and home.

CHAPTER 26

BONFIRE NIGHT

We nearly always had a small bonfire and a few fireworks as one could get a small box of half a dozen fireworks for one shilling and sixpence and quite a few more for a half crown box. Back then fireworks such as Roman Candles cost a shilling each and Catherine Wheels and Bangers even less.

However, when we were teenagers Bonfire Night became a more important event in our lives because my brothers, B and M, were old enough to have Saturday jobs or a paper round and this provided pocket money. B did gardening on Saturday mornings and M did a paper round in the village.

We could not have a really large bonfire in our garden because the vegetable patch furthest away from the house was overhung by a large and beautiful quince tree and the other vegetable patches were either too close to the house or planted with winter greens and sprouts, so we asked the Reeves for permission to have a bonfire in the orchard next to our garden. Although it was an orchard there was a big space where a bonfire could safely be lit.

A great deal of planning and preparation went into it. M did the organising, but always persuaded me to help with the task.

He asked a local farmer for a pile of paper sacks, the kind used to hold animal feed. Newspapers were saved up for weeks beforehand and during the week before Bonfire Night, M and I spent hours scrunching up newspapers into tight balls and stuffing these into the sacks. This was to provide a base for the bonfire. We asked Ernest Reeve for some mangel-wurzels (a root vegetable similar to a sugar beet) which were hollowed out and faces were carved into the front. Candle stubs were placed inside to light up the faces. We also made the guy out of old clothes stuffed with newspaper and with a mangle wurzel for a head.

A few old tree roots were placed at the centre of the bonfire and the sacks of paper placed around them. Once the fire started to burn the tree stumps would burn slowly and hold the heat. John Reeve gave us a whole wagonload of hedge clippings to form the main part of the bonfire.

There were long discussions about which fireworks to buy. My brothers liked Bangers and Jumping Jacks which made loud bangs, or Screech-Owls which sent up a ball of fire into the air and also made a horrible screeching noise. I preferred the pretty fireworks such as Golden Rain or Silver Fountains. B made a list which included Screech Owls, Banshee Wailers, Rockets, Catherine Wheels and Bangers and the boys worked out what they could afford to buy. The cost of fireworks increased each year and pocket money did not go as far as it used to in this respect. Our parents made a small contribution to the fund, but our mother did not really approve of spending too much on fireworks as we did not have much money and Christmas loomed not far ahead.

Several neighbours commented on the bonfire and asked if they could come along to watch the fireworks. John Reeve provided a reserve wagonload of hedge cuttings to add to the bonfire halfway through the evening. John and Ernest had spent several weeks cutting their field hedges back so there was plenty of bonfire material.

As the day grew nearer the weather reports were listened to with great attention and John Reeve's opinion sought if rain threatened. The bonfire had to be held on a Friday or Saturday evening as we all had homework on school evenings and it would be unthinkable in those days to hold a bonfire celebration on a Sunday. We were allowed to ask one or two friends to watch the fireworks.

At last the day dawned bright and clear. We rushed home from the school bus stop after school to change our clothes and get everything ready. I had to wash some baking potatoes which our mother later put into the oven, and lay the table for a quick snack to eat when our mother came home from work. Our father was in charge of the fireworks and had arranged a small display area near the bonfire with a post on which to nail the Catherine wheels and some piping set in the ground from which to launch the rockets. A flat biscuit tin lid nailed on a short post made a platform for the smaller fireworks.

The air was frosty and clear with that wonderful frosty smell, perfect for Bonfire Night. The fire was lit and soon the smoke eddied upwards and permeated the air. The candles were lit in the mangel-wurzels and their faces grinned from the orchard gateposts at anyone passing by. Wrapped up in coats and scarves we gathered in the orchard. The fire had taken hold now and the flames licked up the edges of the bonfire and roared as they attacked the tree stumps further in.

Neighbours and school friends started to arrive and called out greetings to us. Several of them added a handful of fireworks to the carefully covered box which was set well away from the fire or any passing spark. The guy leered at us from its perch at the top of the fire before it was slowly consumed by the flames and collapsed into a smouldering heap. My mother arrived with packets of sparklers which we lit and waved around to make strange patterns in the night air.

Then a rocket burst overhead in a shower of coloured sparks. The main fireworks had begun. Golden rain was succeeded by Roman candles, Screech Owls and Catherine Wheels. Occasional '*oohs*' and '*that's a good 'un*' punctuated the display. The fire gave out an impressive heat so that our fronts were scorched while our backs froze in the evening breeze. We hardly noticed, so intent were we on the fireworks.

There was a short lull while more fireworks were set out and then they began again. Our necks were stiff from gazing upwards at the coloured balls sent up by the Roman Candles which then burst in a shower of coloured light. Mesmerised by the Golden Rain and Silver Fountains which sent out flowing patterns of light like bird feet against the night we hardly noticed our neighbours beside us. John Reeve kept a careful eye on the fire, raking any stray branches back in the centre of the flames. Eventually more hedge clippings were added. The rockets were saved until last and made a glorious burst of coloured light over the orchard.

Then the neighbours, uttering thanks and goodnights, began to drift away. The fire died down though the stumps would burn for some hours. The rest of us returned to our house to eat baked potatoes and sausages, until one by one our schoolfriends were collected. It had been a very special evening.

CHAPTER 27

CAROL SINGING AT LITTLE SOMERFORD

Carol singing was always a magical time for me; a time when there was a real sense of community. A time when the smallest children were carried downstairs to hear us and the oldest villagers were pleased to feel that they had been remembered. We always collected for the village in some way. Our carol singing paid for new curtain material for the village hall, for the teas for the older residents when they went on their annual outing to Weymouth or Bournemouth, or for other worthy causes. Even now, forty years later, villagers still remember our carol singing and bemoan the fact that another village tradition has died out.

My first experience of carol singing was when I was nine years old. My brother M and his friend Nigel from Street Farm were going carol singing and I begged to be allowed to go with them. Another girl called Diane also came with us and we met on The Corner which is the centre of the village. We worked our way down the street singing at a few chosen houses until we came to a large house belonging to Commander and Mrs W.

Commander W was a tall, intimidating man, and his manner rather grand. We trudged up the drive and arranged ourselves in the porch, fumbling with our torches and carol sheets.

'After three,' muttered Nigel and at his command we began to sing the agreed carol.

After one verse Nigel knocked on the door and held out his collecting tin expectantly, but Mrs W ushered us into the large hall. She wanted value for money and expected to hear two or three carols. We arranged ourselves on the hearthrug and began the carol again. We had nearly reached the end of the first verse of *Hark the Herald Angels Sing* when we were interrupted by an extremely loud braying noise which was meant to be singing, followed by a splash.

Our singing faltered, but we re-gathered our strength and continued for another line or two. The bathroom was off the hall and the loud braying noise came again, a very loud tuneless 'tum te tum de daaaah daaaah' sung by someone who was clearly tone deaf. This was so unlike herald angels that I started to giggle.

M stepped on my foot and jabbed me sharply in the ribs with his elbow and we carried on, but when the raucous noise started again I was not the only one who burst into giggles.

'Shush,' muttered M, biting back his laughter, 'she's coming back.'

Stifling their laughter and not daring to look each other in the eye, the other three carried on. I had to bite the inside of my mouth until it bled to stop myself laughing.

Mrs W, who had gone into the kitchen to fetch her purse, returned saying, 'I'm *terribly* sorry, I *do* hope you don't mind. I'm afraid Humphrey *always* sings in his bath and he's rather *deaf.* Do carry on.' We started the final verse but just as we had sung: *Hark the herald angels* … we heard the tuneless braying even louder than before, accompanied by loud splashing. This was too much for us and we were unable to smother our laughter.

Mrs W was rather embarrassed, I think, because she only put one penny in our tin and ushered us outside as quickly as possible. We raced to the end of the drive and laughed and laughed. I was never in awe of Commander W again, and to this day I can't hear this lovely carol without smiling as I think of this episode.

The next year or two I went with my friend, Wendy Barnes, and her mother, Stella. We visited only the main village houses as Mrs Barnes could only take us on one or two nights and the village was quite spread out.

From the age of about thirteen I started organising the carol singing myself. It was planned over four or five nights and we stopped at every house, usually ending up somewhere where refreshments were provided while we counted the night's takings. Everyone knew we were collecting for the village. Old people who lived alone were informed beforehand when we would be coming so that they would not be worried about shuffling noises outside their front doors after dark. The postmaster,

Mr Tyzack, who also delivered the post, would convey messages.

'You have to go to Colonel Brassey's on Tuesday,' he would say, or 'If you go to the Mill on Thursday, they're having a party and there'll be more people to put money in your tin' or 'Mrs Porter says if you go on Wednesday at 7.30, she'll have some mince pies for you.'

There were only a handful of young people in the village, so almost everyone of a suitable age was persuaded to come along. If smaller children were desperate to join in they were allowed out for an hour and then escorted home. On one occasion an eleven year old girl reported that her friend was not coming because they had quarrelled; she related the rude remark her friend had made.

'Oh dear,' I said, 'What did you say to her?'

'Us told 'er to go away and pee down 'er leg!' came the unforgettable reply.

The weather often determined the route. The main street and the housing estate in the centre of the village were reserved for the evenings when freezing fog made wandering along country lanes dangerous in the dark. The first night we would visit the houses on The Hill and some in The Street, ending up at Mrs Hilda Porter's house where we were always made welcome and asked in for mince pies, sausage rolls and orange squash.

On one occasion we were singing outside the living room window of a house on The Hill, and suddenly the curtains were drawn back and the window opened a little by Mr Thomas, one of the older villagers, and we saw Mrs Thomas propped up in bed in her living room. The poor lady was rather unwell at that time, but she was so pleased to see us, and requested two of her favourite carols. It was clear that it would be her last Christmas and tears shone in their eyes, and mine too, for they were much loved in the village.

One evening, after singing at all the houses on the estate we would trudge up East End Lane to the two farms and two houses at the top. We would wander back in the moonlight, our breath clouding in the frosty air as we listened to the distant hooting of tawny owls which we would imitate by blowing through our frozen fingers.

The following night we would visit the houses further down the main street and go on to the council houses and sometimes to The Rectory at Great Somerford since Mr Pelham was our rector too. We would return to Manor Farm where Colonel (later Sir Hugh) and Mrs Brassey and their grown up family would welcome us in for refreshments and chat to us.

A little later we counted the money we had received that evening and on the way home I would drop off the money at the post office where Mr Tyzack put it in the safe. Most of the villagers were very generous and the older people handed out toffees and were keen to learn the names of the 'new' children from the estate.

One man, Mr X, who lived in the centre of the village, once asked 'What will I get if I put sixpence in your tin?'

I was astonished, but managed to say: 'You'll get a free tea; we're collecting for the Over Sixties' outing.'

This piece of news went round the village at the speed

of light and over the next few days everyone was stopping me in the street to ask me if Mr X had *really* said that! The kinder ones usually remarking afterwards that Mr X was not known for his generosity, but they didn't know that he was as bad as *that*, but most people gasping in amazement 'The ole skinflint!'

Somebody must have said something to Mr X because he planned revenge. The post office was the place where all village gossip was exchanged, discussed, pronounced upon and relayed back around the village within minutes, so Mr X went to the post office and stated that we were keeping the money we had collected.

Mr Tyzack, the Postmaster, was furious because he was looking after our money and one of his own children was a carol singer. He fetched our bag of money from the safe and slammed it down on the counter in front of Mr X in fury.

'Here's the carol singing money!' he bellowed, *'In my safe!'*

Later he came to find me to tell me what Mr X was saying. 'Nobody's goin' ter believe 'im; I'll soon put 'em right. The cheek!' he added indignantly. 'Don't you worry! I gave 'im a piece've my mind! I nearly *thumped* 'im; 'e won't come back 'ere in a hurry I tell you!'

One moonlit evening a few of us walked down the lonely road to Kingsmead Mill. There was a sharp frost and the moon shed a cold light over the hoary fields. An almost unnatural stillness hung over everything giving the soft landscape an ethereal beauty. It was so bright we didn't need torches and the lane glimmered in front of us highlighted by the frost.

Suddenly a dark figure stepped out of the hedgerow a few yards in front of us and stood in the road blocking our way. My heart lurched in fright; I was the eldest and responsible for several younger children. I was hastily thinking of possible escape routes over the fields when the figure spoke and I breathed a sigh of relief as I recognised my brother, M.

I suspect that my mother sent him along as Mill Lane is rather lonely in the dark and I was very grateful to have his company. We walked on to Kingsmead Mill where we had a job to make ourselves heard as the mill race was roaring behind us and a lively party was in progress in an upper room. Suddenly the windows were flung open, the music turned low and several guests came down to join in the carols. One of the guests took our collecting tin to pass it around inside and we were grateful for their generosity.

On Christmas Eve we always went carol singing at the pub which was The Three Crowns; it is now called The Somerford Arms, or The Somerfords as the villagers call it. Although children were not supposed to go in the bar, we were allowed just inside for the occasion and we crept shyly into the room. There was a strong smell of beer, cigarette smoke clouded the air and everyone was talking loudly around the bar.

'Oi, Bert, turn that juke box off will you; it's the carol singers!' someone would call out and slowly the chatter would die down.

'I've already put money in their tin,' grumbled one man.

'Oh, get away with you,' retorted the lady next to him. 'We've all put money in the tin, but they're collecting for the village. Anyway it's Christmas and we can all find a few more pennies.'

So he was shouted down and everyone would join in our carol before dropping money into our collecting tin. In the hearty chorus of 'Zoi-lent, noight, 'Ooly noight' sung in broad Wiltshire accents by the people of my beloved village I felt a real sense of community.

POSTSCRIPT

TIMES CHANGE

It is curious to know that back in the 1950s and 1960s we were far ahead of our time in the way we lived.

Nowadays it is fashionable to eat organic food and to lower one's carbon footprint by buying local produce and eating fruit and vegetables in season. We did this as a way of life.

Our father read the *New Scientist* and cautioned against any use of carcinogenic pesticides on our vegetable patch, so nothing was sprayed and slugs and caterpillars had to be picked off cabbages and lettuces by hand. We did not usually buy fruit and vegetables unless our garden supply had been used up, or unless it was an occasional orange or banana which we could not grow ourselves. If money was short we went without, often having two weeks of plenty after our mother's pay day, followed by two weeks when food was scarce because bills had to be paid. I particularly remember one occasion when the five of us existed for a week on one jar of home-made apple chutney, the last in the larder, and a loaf of sliced bread. There were eighteen slices in that loaf, I chose the thin-sliced loaf in the shop because it had the most slices. That was three and a half slices each for the week. Of course intermittent fasting has become very fashionable. Remember that we started the trend back in the 1960s.

Our parents told us that many people visited the countryside for their holidays and since we already lived there we did not need to go away. We hardly ever travelled beyond Malmesbury, except for the annual school outing, until we were in our late teens and went off on archaeological digs to earn some money.

I recently stayed in a four star hotel where the carpet had been removed from the bedrooms in order to update the décor. It forcibly reminded me of the bare floorboards in my childhood bedroom. No one, I thought, would embrace that idea if they had lived through the bitter winter of 1962—3, with deep snow outside, no upstairs heating and thick ice on the inside of the bedroom windows.

Nearly every time I pick up a newspaper there is an article on the wonderful new trend of buying one's clothes from charity shops. After years of being teased at grammar school over ill-fitting second-hand clothes, or four inch tucks in the sleeves of my 'blouses' which were really hand-me-down shirts from my brothers, and which some more fortunate girls were keen to point out, didn't even button up on the correct side, this is not a trend which appeals to me.

In the 1960s, girls did not have the pressures of social media and the constant air-brushed photos of celebrities to compete with. It was bad enough back then having brothers who compared my teenage spots to the constellations and who had long discussions at the supper table as to whether it was The Plough or Orion they could see in my complexion that day!

Our carbon footprint was almost non-existent in those days living in a house with no bathroom, no hot water on tap, no washing machine, television, telephone or car. Although life was often hard and despite having to go without many things which people today would consider necessities, I do think that life was in many ways better, partly because children could play out and about in comparative safety as villagers looked out for them.

Children were encouraged to behave as they knew that any misbehaviour would be reported to their parents within minutes.

At the time we knew it, Little Somerford was an identifiable rural community with its own customs and characters. The people had retained their individuality. They were not subject to such influences as the media and the car in the way that they are today. Village life, as it always had done, revolved around the school, the shop, church, village hall and Somerford Show. This created a close-knit community.

I feel privileged to have known these village people. Their kindness and friendliness gave us a sense of belonging, a sense of community, and a connection to the landscape which I have never felt elsewhere, and life was better for it.

ACKNOWLEDGEMENTS

My sincere and grateful thanks to the following people:

Lorna Brookes of Crumps Barn Studio who has been immensely helpful. Thank you for having confidence in my writing.

Dr Charles Moseley, Life Fellow, Hughes Hall, Cambridge, for reading my manuscript, making encouraging comments and giving kind advice.

Andrew Walkland for reading the manuscript, editing mistakes and suggesting clarification where necessary.

Basil Abbott for reading some parts of the manuscript and encouraging me to continue with it.

Special thanks to Christine Sparrow and Wendy Garside who attended Little Somerford School with me and who allowed me to write about them and their families.

Also Eileen Webb, another friend from childhood, who read the pieces on The Shop and Little Somerford School and then thanked me for reviving so many childhood memories.

Old friends from Little Somerford who deserve great

thanks for reading and approving parts of the manuscript where I mentioned them or their parents. I am so grateful to be able to include these memories.

These include Martyn and Pauline Scott, who were always helpful and encouraging. They read most of the manuscript and Martyn supplied the photos of the snow on The Hill in 1963.

Robert and Julie Gawthropp who allowed me to include my memories of Cecil and Kathleeen Gawthropp.

Julie Frayling also supplied one or two photos.

Christopher Stoneham, who approved the piece about Edith Stoneham.

Oliver Jones-Davies for allowing me to take a photo of Yew Tree Farm.

Francis Chamberlain who was very helpful and allowed me to include some memories of his family.

Love and thanks to our old friend Jean Boulton, who enjoyed reading my memories of her mother Mrs Isles, and her uncles: George Isles and Frank Knight, and at the grand old age of ninety-nine, wrote me an eight page hand written letter in response to reading my piece on Little Somerford School which she had attended herself.

Thanks to my brothers who sent me documents and photos of the Reeve family.

Finally, my special love and thanks to my husband, John, who has read the manuscript more than once, made positive comments, and listened to endless stories about the village.

In my last conversation with my mother, Eve Viner, who died in 2019 aged 95, she confirmed my memories of the Frogspawn incident, and my brother M shutting me in the stable with the carthorse at Union Farm. I am thankful that I inherited her wonderful memory.